MARK

FORTRESS COMMENTARY ON THE BIBLE

Fortress Commentary on the Bible: The Old Testament and Apocrypha
Fortress Commentary on the Bible: The New Testament
The Pentateuch: Fortress Commentary on the Bible Study Edition
The Prophets: Fortress Commentary on the Bible Study Edition
Wisdom, Worship, and Poetry: Fortress Commentary on the Bible Study Edition
The Historical Writings: Fortress Commentary on the Bible Study Edition
The Gospels and Acts: Fortress Commentary on the Bible Study Edition
The Letters and Legacy of Paul: Fortress Commentary on the Bible Study Edition
Hebrews, the General Epistles, and Revelation: Fortress Commentary on the Bible Study Edition
1 and 2 Kings: Fortress Commentary on the Bible
Isaiah: Fortress Commentary on the Bible
Mark: Fortress Commentary on the Bible
1 and 2 Corinthians: Fortress Commentary on the Bible

MARK

FORTRESS COMMENTARY ON THE BIBLE

RAQUEL S. LETTSOME

FORTRESS PRESS
Minneapolis

MARK
Fortress Commentary on the Bible

31 30 29 28 27 26 25 1 2 3 4 5 6 7 8 9

Library of Congress Cataloging-in-Publication Data

Names: Lettsome, Raquel S., author
Title: Mark : Fortress commentary on the Bible / Raquel S. Lettsome.
Description: Minneapolis : Fortress Press, [2026]
Identifiers: LCCN 2025035430 (print) | LCCN 2025035431 (ebook) | ISBN 9798341900134 paperback | ISBN 9798341900141 ebook
Subjects: LCSH: Bible. Mark--Commentaries
Classification: LCC BS2585.53 .L48 2026 (print) | LCC BS2585.53 (ebook)
LC record available at https://lccn.loc.gov/2025035430
LC ebook record available at https://lccn.loc.gov/2025035431

Cover design: Kris E. Miller
Cover image: compilation of stock textures from Getty Images

Print ISBN: 979-8-3419-0013-4
eBook ISBN: 979-8-3419-0014-1

CONTENTS

CONTRIBUTORS

Raquel S. Lettsome
Itinerant Elder
African Methodist Episcopal Church

Volume Editors

Margaret Aymer
Associate Professor of New Testament and Chair of Biblical Studies
Interdenominational Theological Center

Cynthia Briggs Kittredge
Dean and President and Professor of New Testament
Seminary of the Southwest

David A. Sánchez
Associate Professor of Theological Studies
Loyola Marymount University

ABBREVIATIONS

General

AT	Alpha Text (of the Greek text of Esther)
BOI	Book of Isaiah
Chr	Chronicler
DH	Deuteronomistic History
DI	Deutero-Isaiah
Dtr	Deuteronomist
Gk.	Greek
H	Holiness Code
Heb.	Hebrew
JPS	Jewish Publication Society
LXX	The Septuagint
LXX B	Vaticanus Text of the Septuagint
MP	Mode of production
MT	Masoretic Text
NIV	New International Version
NRSV	New Revised Standard Version
OAN	Oracles against Nations (in Jeremiah)
P.	papyrus/papyri
P	Priestly source
PE	Pastoral Epistles
RSV	Revised Standard Version
TI	Trito-Isaiah

Books of the Bible (NT, OT, Apocrypha)

Old Testament/Hebrew Bible

Gen.	Genesis
Exod.	Exodus
Lev.	Leviticus
Num.	Numbers
Deut.	Deuteronomy
Josh.	Joshua
Judg.	Judges
Ruth	Ruth
1 Sam.	1 Samuel
2 Sam.	2 Samuel
1 Kgs.	1 Kings
2 Kgs.	2 Kings
1 Chron.	1 Chronicles
2 Chron.	2 Chronicles
Ezra	Ezra
Neh.	Nehemiah
Esther	Esther
Job	Job
Ps. (Pss.)	Psalms
Prov.	Proverbs
Eccles.	Ecclesiastes
Song.	Song of Songs
Isa.	Isaiah
Jer.	Jeremiah
Lam.	Lamentations
Ezek.	Ezekiel
Dan.	Daniel
Hosea	Hosea
Joel	Joel
Amos	Amos
Obad.	Obadiah
Jon.	Jonah
Mic.	Micah
Nah.	Nahum
Hab.	Habakkuk
Zeph.	Zephaniah

Hag.	Haggai
Zech.	Zechariah
Mal.	Malachi

Apocrypha

Tob.	Tobit
Jth.	Judith
Gk. Esther	Greek Additions to Esther
Sir.	Sirach (Ecclesiasticus)
Bar.	Baruch
Let. Jer.	Letter of Jeremiah
Add Dan.	Additions to Daniel
Pr. Azar.	Prayer of Azariah
Sg. Three.	Song of the Three Young Men (or Three Jews)
Sus.	Susanna
Bel	Bel and the Dragon
1 Macc.	1 Maccabees
2 Macc.	2 Maccabees
1 Esd.	1 Esdras
Pr. of Man.	Prayer of Manasseh
2 Esd.	2 Esdras
Wis.	Wisdom of Solomon
3 Macc.	3 Maccabees
4 Macc.	4 Maccabees

New Testament

Matt.	Matthew
Mark	Mark
Luke	Luke
John	John
Acts	Acts of the Apostles
Rom.	Romans
1 Cor.	1 Corinthians
2 Cor.	2 Corinthians
Gal.	Galatians
Eph.	Ephesians
Phil.	Philippians

Col.	Colossians
1 Thess.	1 Thessalonians
2 Thess.	2 Thessalonians
1 Tim.	1 Timothy
2 Tim.	2 Timothy
Titus	Titus
Philem.	Philemon
Heb.	Hebrews
James	James
1 Pet.	1 Peter
2 Pet.	2 Peter
1 John	1 John
2 John	2 John
3 John	3 John
Jude	Jude
Rev.	Revelation (Apocalypse)

Journals, Series, Reference Works

ABD	*Anchor Bible Dictionary*. Edited by David Noel Freedman. 6 vols. New York: Doubleday, 1992.
BTB	*Biblical Theology Bulletin*
CBQMS	Catholic Biblical Quarterly Monograph Series
JBL	*Journal of Biblical Literature*
NovT	*Novum Testamentum*
WW	*Word and World*

Ancient Authors and Texts

Eusebius of Caesarea

Hist. eccl.	*Historia ecclesiastica*

Mark

Introduction

No one knows exactly who wrote the Gospel of Mark. The ancient church historian Eusebius wrote that Bishop Papias of Asia Minor attributed the Gospel to John Mark (Acts 12:12; Col. 4:10), who was a follower and interpreter of Peter (*Hist. eccl.* 3.39). This would suggest that it was not a firsthand account of Jesus' ministry. The general consensus is that Mark, whoever he may be, wrote the Gospel somewhere in the Roman Empire between 66 and 70 CE. The precise dating of the Gospel hinges on the interpretation of the events prophesied by Jesus in Mark 13. For some scholars, the similarity between Jesus' prediction that there will be left of the temple "no stone upon a stone" and Josephus's narrative of the temple being razed in 70 suggests that Mark should be dated after the fall of the temple (Marcus; Pesch; Theissen). I find this a compelling argument (St. Clair). Therefore, the context of Mark's Gospel is the Jewish War: It is one of several Jewish and Christian responses to the fall of the temple.

The setting first posited for Mark's Gospel was Rome. This is where John Mark was believed to have written it, according to Papias. But the Gospel's use of Latin involves only a few military terms like "legion" (5:9) and "centurion" (15:39); there are no Latin words that reflect the social, domestic, or religious areas of Roman life (Kelber, 129). Based on this evidence, it is more probable that Mark wrote somewhere in the Roman Empire other than in Rome itself. Scholars have since identified Galilee and southern Syria as possible locales, suggestions that would also disqualify John Mark as the author. The viability of each of these locations primarily depends on how well they account for certain characteristics of Mark's Gospel: geographical discrepancies (his knowledge of the Galilean locales is lacking beyond their names, and his topology is often inaccurate: 1977); the use of a number of Hebrew (7:11; 11:9) and Aramaic words in transliteration (5:41; 7:34; 14:36; 15:22, 34), most of them translated into Greek, suggesting that Mark's community included Jews and gentiles in close association (Waetjen, 14); the explanation of Jewish traditions (e.g., 7:3–4) to at least some readers unfamiliar with them; the author's and presumed audience's familiarity with Jewish Scriptures, which are cited on twelve occasions, without further explanation (1:2–3; 4:12; 7:6–7; 10:6–8, 19; 11:17; 12:10–11, 36; 13:24–26; 14:27, 62; 15:34); and the representation of Jesus' ministry to gentiles, suggesting the presence of some gentiles, at least, in the audience. Both Rome and southern Syria had large gentile populations with a significant number of Jewish inhabitants, but given the limited use of Latinisms mentioned above, southern Syria seems more probable. Moreover, the Gospel's setting seems to be more rural than urban. All of Jesus' parables use agrarian imagery, and the majority of Jesus' ministry occurs in the villages, towns, farms, and countryside (1:38; 6:56; 8:27; 11:1, 2, 11, 12; 14:3).

Until the 1800s, Mark's Gospel was neglected, for the most part, by both church tradition and scholarship because it was not a firsthand account and because it was dated after Matthew (Catholic scholars) or after both Matthew and Luke (Protestant scholars). Nevertheless, it boasts some unique literary features. The author highlights key points and narrative themes by "sandwiching" one story in the middle of another, arranging episodes into concentric patterns, using two similar stories to begin and end a large section of the Gospel (Rhoads, Dewey, and Michie 1999). Mark's style is terse and literal. This led Augustine to conclude that Mark was an abbreviated version of Matthew. It was not until 1838 that Mark's priority was established (by C. J. Wilkes and C. H. Weisse). Mark's Gospel then gained popularity because its simplistic style suggested historical accuracy, until form critics argued that the Gospel was not historically accurate but reflected the beliefs of early Christian communities. They examined the literary units to reveal the *Sitz im Leben* of the various forms in the Gospel. Next, the redaction critics focused on the author's arrangement of the tradition, thereby uncovering the author's theological approach to it.

Interest in the Gospel shifted from the historical to the literary. Mark was then primarily viewed as narrative, understood as a "communication event between a writer and an audience" (Juel, 13). The narrative approach to the Gospel drew attention to the contemporary audience or reader and how they engaged the text. This brought to the fore theological concerns that are of importance to people in local churches, rather than only literary and historical issues (Placher, ix–xi). Contemporary Mark scholarship examines the traditional themes of discipleship, Christology, and kingdom of God in the text. However, these are now reexamined through different cultural and theological lenses to expose the liberative strains of Mark's Gospel.

Mark 1:1–13

The Beginning of the Good News

The Text in Its Ancient Context

According to Mark, his story is "good news" (*euangelion*). Although his tidings of "good news" announce a beginning, they do not stand as an isolated experience. Rather, he connects his story to the story of Israel. Moreover, the content of his story will not focus on a single event but on a singular person: Jesus, whom he labels as both "Christ" and "Son of God." For those in his audience who are familiar with the Hebrew Scriptures, the title Christ brings to fore communal memories of exile and foreign rule under Babylon and subsequent deliverance under Cyrus. According to Isa. 44:28, Cyrus was God's anointed (*christos*), and his release of the captives was seen by Isaiah as a result of God's intervention. By employing the designation "Christ," Mark identifies Jesus as the anointed of God who will be used for a divine purpose. In the context of first-century Palestine languishing under foreign (Roman) rule, it would be hard to walk away from these opening lines without having expectations of deliverance raised. Mark compounds this further by his use of "Son of God." Jesus is more than God's anointed; he is in fact God's Son. Textual experts disagree about whether this title in Mark 1:1 is part of Mark's original text or a later inclusion. The title is missing from a few important manuscripts (e.g., Sinaiticus) and present in others (e.g., Vaticanus). However, the presence of the title in important manuscripts like Vaticanus, along with Mark's penchant for identifying Jesus as God's Son throughout the Gospel (1:11; 3:11; 5:7; 9:7; 12:6; 13:32; 14:61; 15:39), suggests that its inclusion here is the work of an omniscient narrator clearly stating his point of view from the start.

Against the backdrop of Old Testament prophecy, Mark sets the stage for the events that follow. Although he opens with a quote that he ascribes to Isaiah (1:2), the first portion of the quotation ("I am sending a messenger ahead of you") is better attributed to Exod. 23:20 and Mal. 3:1. Exodus 23:20 evokes images of wilderness wanderings in which God sends forth a messenger (*angelos*) to keep watch over the Israelites as they sojourn to the promised land. Malachi 3:1 describes the sending of the messenger prior to the coming of the Day of the Lord. The second portion of the quotation, found in Isa. 40:3 (Mark 1:3), announces the coming of the Lord but without the tones of impending judgment found in Malachi. Instead of condemnation, the prophet heralds the end of the exile and Babylonian captivity.

By detailing both John's proclamation and performance against the landscape of Old Testament prophecy, Mark conveys a sense of hope and expectancy to his original readers. As an introduction to his work, this citation of the prophets implicitly offers the theme of judgment as a means of understanding the destruction of the Jerusalem temple by the Romans and unites it here with a theme of comfort. Just as John preaches and baptizes in preparation of the Lord's arrival (1:3, 7–8), so Mark sets the narrative stage for Jesus' appearance.

The narrative lens then turns to Jesus, who has come to the Jordan to be baptized by John. Mark has already introduced him as "Christ" and, depending on how one interprets the textual evidence for Mark

1:1, also "Son of God," perhaps to counter any negative preconceived notions that his audience may have about the next bit of information that he shares. Jesus is from Nazareth of Galilee, a small village off the main roads that is about seventy miles from Jerusalem. Jesus' hometown has no geographic, religious, or political importance of its own. However, about four miles northwest lies the city of Sepphoris. Not only was Sepphoris highly influenced by Rome, but it also greatly angered the rest of Galilee when it refused to rebel against Rome in 66 CE. Had not Mark given the titles in the first verse, his audience's initial perception of Jesus might be as a "nobody from nowhere," or worse, a Roman sympathizer. The titles "Christ" and "Son of God" help to persuade his readers that it is his personage rather than his address that is significant.

Mark tells us nothing of Jesus prior to this moment. It seems that his baptism is the beginning of his story and nothing before matters. The heavens, the barrier separating the human and divine realms, are torn. The Greek verb, *schizein*, suggests that the tear is irreparable. There will be no mending of this breach: God is now accessible to human beings and human beings are accessible to God (Juel, 34–35). Through this divide comes the Spirit in the form of a dove, perhaps intimating the birth of a new creation (Gen. 1:2; 8:8). Mark notes that the dove descends "into" (*eis*) him—not "upon" (*epi*) him (Matt. 3:16; Luke 3:22). Jesus is indwelled by the Spirit. Finally, a voice speaks from heaven affirming that he is God's Son, who is both "pleasing" and "well loved."

No sooner does the Spirit descend into Jesus than it "drives" him into the wilderness. Jesus is cast out from human company, much like the demons he will cast out in his ministry. Both his location and length of stay are important to note. They allude to the children of Israel's sojourn in the wilderness for forty years. Jesus is also in a place of testing, suggesting that his departure from this place will be the fulfillment of another divine promise. However, it will not be without opposition. Otherworldly lines of demarcation are being drawn: Satan tests him and angels minister to him, leaving his audience to wonder how this will play out in the human realm.

The Text in the Interpretive Tradition

Questions about Jesus' (divine and/or human) nature have caused Mark's account of Jesus' baptism to be ignored and/or conflated with Matthew's version. Until the late eighteenth century, Matthew was believed to be the first written Gospel. According to Augustine, Mark was Matthew's abbreviator. Therefore, Matthew's Gospel, which included an infancy narrative and an explanation of why Jesus was being baptized (Matt. 3:14), was preferred. Once Markan priority was established, it became clear that the early church had been uncomfortable with Mark's presentation and preferred Matthew, often called the "church's Gospel," because it corrected Mark's lack of episodes such as the infancy narrative, which depicts the miraculous nature of Jesus' birth, and the lack of explanation for Jesus' receiving John's "baptism of repentance," which implicitly called into question early Christian belief in Jesus' sinlessness.

Rather than focus on what this passage says about Jesus' (divine or human) nature, contemporary scholars explore the connection between Jesus' baptism and his ministry. His baptism is understood as Jesus' surrender to God's will, his divine commissioning by God, his rejection of the dominant culture, and/or his identification with sinners. Questions of divine origin hinge more on whether "Son of God" (1:1) was originally included in Mark's manuscript than on an examination of Mark's baptism account alone.

The Text in Contemporary Discussion

If we are to follow the trajectory of contemporary scholars and focus on Jesus' ministry, baptism becomes intimately connected to discipleship. We can no longer stop with the question of who Jesus is but must ask, how can others follow him? Matthew, Mark, and Luke record John's proclaiming a "baptism of repentance." It may be helpful for readers of Mark's Gospel to think about repentance as changing one's heart or mind and then read the Gospel with this question in mind: How does

Mark's story of Jesus get us to change our minds about the world around us and our participation in it?

Mark 1:14–39

An Invitation to Follow

The Text in Its Ancient Context

Unlike John, who ministered in the southern region of Judea near the urban center of Jerusalem, Jesus' ministry begins in the northern region of Galilee. Galilee was known for its farming and fishing, both industries sustained through the labor of a predominantly peasant population. It was a largely rural area surrounded by foreign nations whose inhabitants would later be strongly resistant to the Romans during the war (66-70 CE). They reaped none of the benefits Rome bestowed on the Jewish political and religious elites in the south. Instead, their labor fueled an economy that kept them at the lowest economic and social strata of ancient Palestinian society. It is here that Jesus proclaims the impending arrival of God's kingdom.

The first thing Mark shows his community is that the kingdom has both social and economic implications. As Jesus "pass[es] along" the Sea of Galilee, he calls four fishermen to follow him: Simon, Andrew, James, and John (vv. 16–20). Each of them responds without hesitation. They leave behind all ties to their current livelihood, which will affect them economically and affect their relationships with their families. James and John work with their father, Zebedee. We will soon see that Simon is married; he has a mother-in-law (v. 30). If we are to begin to understand the appeal of Jesus' invitation, we must first refrain from equating the modern industry of fishing and our understanding of entrepreneurship with the profession in its ancient Palestinian form. According to K. C. Hanson, the fishing industry was highly regulated and governed by political and kinship ties. The profits routinely made their way to the coffers of the urban elites, leaving many fishermen indebted to brokers for leases and money needed to run their businesses. Fisherman often formed cooperatives to survive. If they did not have enough people in the cooperative, they hired laborers, as Zebedee did (Hanson, 104). In effect, the four men forsake the highly regulated vocation that is controlled by the Jewish elites and accept Jesus' invitation to follow and fish for people.

Next, Mark demonstrates that the kingdom of God is manifest in both Jesus' word and deed (vv. 21–18). When Jesus enters the synagogue and begins to teach, he astonishes the audience with the level of authority he possesses. In the midst of his teaching, a man with an unclean spirit interrupts him and identifies him as the "Holy One of God." The presence of the man is not surprising: the world was believed to be inhabited by spirits, which were mainly malevolent in nature. Both Judaism and the pagan religions of the Greco-Roman world saw the need for people to be freed from the power of unclean spirits/demons. In Judaism, the presence of unclean spirits symbolized the struggle between God and the forces of evil (Mann). Therefore it is ironic that the people who are supposed to be on the side of God, namely, the religious leaders and members of the congregation, are not the first characters in Mark's narrative to recognize who Jesus really is. Instead, it is the unclean spirit who knows what the people of God do not. Jesus responds by silencing and exorcizing the demon with a verbal command, thereby confirming the audience's original assessment of his authoritative teaching. His is a "performative utterance" (Tolbert). Jesus speaks and things happen; demons obey.

Finally, kingdom life involves service. Jesus and his four followers return to Simon's house, where they find Simon's mother-in-law sick with a fever. Jesus takes her by the hand and heals her of the fever. In return, she begins to serve them. She is the second character in Mark's story to serve (*diakonein*) Jesus; the first are the angels in the wilderness (1:13). These acts of service foreshadow Jesus' teaching and example of discipleship as servanthood (10:43, 45).

The Text in the Interpretive Tradition

As early as the Middle Ages, the church interpreted the kingdom (*basileia*) of God as a sphere of influence (reign of God) rather than a spatial reality (physical kingdom). However, they equated God's reign with ecclesial rule (Mann). In the mid-1800s, Albrecht Ritschl awakened scholarly interest in this theological concept. He argued that the kingdom of God was the sociopolitical transformation of this world and that it would result in the overthrow of oppression. His work laid the foundation for the social gospel movement, which peaked in the early 1900s. However, Ritschl's work lacked the apocalyptic edge that other scholars believed was present in the Gospel's articulation of the kingdom of God. Scholars such as Johannes Weiss, Albert Schweitzer, and Rudolf Bultmann maintained the apocalyptic notion of time that is divided into two eras: the now and the not yet. For these scholars, the kingdom is a future reality that is beyond human control. C. H. Dodd rejected this otherworldly, future orientation and advocated a realized eschatology. For him, the kingdom of God was already present whenever and wherever God's rule was established.

In the mid-1900s, the next wave of scholarship sought to mediate between the apocalyptic and realized eschatological thrusts of kingdom language. They attempted to bridge the academic chasm between the now and the not-yet, on the one hand, and the kingdom as beyond human control and the participatory nature of the kingdom, on the other (Blount). In addition, scholars moved away from a "pan-Synoptic" approach to the kingdom, in which they studied the kingdom-of-God concept across the Gospels. Instead, they began to explore how individual Gospels presented the kingdom of God (France). Liberation theologians who have equated the kingdom with sociopolitical acts of liberation have taken the symbol full circle, bringing scholarship back to the groundbreaking work of Ritschl as well as to its critiques (Blount).

The Text in Contemporary Discussion

During the last few years, the emerging church movement, which has been defined as "a growing, loosely-connected movement of primarily young pastors who are glad to see the end of modernity and are seeking to function as missionaries who bring the gospel of Jesus Christ to emerging and postmodern cultures" (Driscoll 2006, 22), has shown renewed interest in the kingdom of God. They claim that the kingdom of God is, or at least can be, here and now: "Our [principal] desire is to see God's kingdom come on earth as it is in heaven. We believe this happens when God's people are renewed around God's mission of love and justice in the world" (Maddock and Maddock, 80). This mission of love and justice in the world includes addressing ecological, moral, economic, and social ills. The focus is, therefore, communal, as relationships are of primary importance. However, it is not only human relationships that matter but also humanity's relationship with all of creation.

The communal emphasis of the emerging church movement is similar to that of liberation theologians, who see the redistribution of wealth and a sociopolitical reordering of society that brings in those who have been relegated to the margins as part of the kingdom of God agenda. However, liberation theologians believe that the presence of evil is so pervasive that the kingdom agenda as they understand it cannot be brought about completely by human initiative. It will require divine intervention for its fulfillment, including judgment on those people and systems that oppose God's work. For the emerging church movement, the future is bright. Heaven will eventually come to earth as the kingdom of God is manifested through good works.

As we read Mark's presentation of Jesus' proclamation of the kingdom and Jesus' ministry, how are we to articulate its meaning in a postmodern setting? However we define it, we must be mindful that our definitions have implications for both mission and eschatology.

Mark 1:40–3:6

Following beyond the Boundaries

The Text in Its Ancient Context

Jesus' ministry in Galilee continues to grow. However, it brings to him not only the crowds but also the criticism of the scribes and Pharisees.

Mark's presentation of Jesus' ministry and the response of the religious leadership in Galilee show a fundamental difference between the two. By narrating a series of boundary-crossing ministry acts in a concentric pattern, Mark highlights for his audience both the growing tensions between Jesus and the religious leaders in Galilee and the reasons for Jesus' popularity among people in the region.

The first episode in this section (1:40–45) reveals that Jesus' fame has now reached the lowest social strata—the outcasts. A leper approaches Jesus. Despite the hopelessness of his situation, he does not question Jesus' ability to cleanse him. The only barrier the leper perceives to his deliverance is Jesus' willingness to cross the boundaries of ritual purity in order to engage and aid him. Jesus is willing and sends the cleansed man to the priests, commanding that he offer what Moses commanded in the law (Lev. 14:1–7). The leper does not do as Jesus commands, however, but instead tells what Jesus has done for him. Jesus' fame increases to the point that he cannot go into the town but must remain in the country.

As Jesus' popularity grows, so does his conflict with the religious leaders in Galilee. In the remainder of this section of his Gospel (2:1–3:6), Mark shows this by setting up these stories in a series of concentric circles (Rhoads, Dewey, and Michie, 52). He frames this section with two healing stories (2:1–12 and 3:1–6) placed at the beginning and end of this section. The first pericope details the healing of a paralytic. Jesus heals the man so that the scribes who accuse him of blasphemy will know "that the Son of Man has authority on earth to forgive sins" (2:10). In the last, he heals a man with a withered hand. It appears to be a setup since "they watched to see whether he would cure him on the sabbath, so that they might accuse him" (3:2). In both passages, Jesus' power, his "ability to exercise control over the behavior of others" (Pilch, 139), is unquestionable. He has the power to affect the functioning of both men's bodies. The real issue is Jesus' authority, whether he has the "socially recognized and approved ability to control the behavior of others" (Malina, 11). The scribes in 2:1–12 and the Pharisees and Herodians in 3:1–6 do not believe Jesus has the authority to forgive sin or transgress Sabbath law just because he has the power to heal. They do not share the same willingness demonstrated by Jesus when he healed the leper: a willingness to use both power and authority to help those in need. Therefore, Mark shows his audience that if things are left up to the current religious leadership, nothing will change for the vast majority of people.

The second and fourth episodes deal with eating regulations (2:13–17 and 2:23–28). In the second episode, Jesus calls a tax collector by the name of Levi to follow him. Later that evening, he is eating with Levi and many tax collectors and sinners are eating with them. Although the tax collectors represent an economically stable cadre of individuals, they were considered social outcasts and the greatest sinners. They were exploiters of the common people; they raised funds that supported the oppressive regimes of Herod and Rome. Moreover, they increased their salaries by extorting from the people additional money in excess of the tax rate. At first glance, Mark's audience might get the impression that Jesus' table fellowship with tax collectors and sinners implies his approval of them. However, Mark makes it clear to his readers, just as Jesus makes it clear to the scribes that question him, that Jesus is calling sinners because they are the ones in need of assistance. His ministry is directed to those outside the pale of Jewish law, and he goes where they are in order to get them.

The fourth pericope also has to do with eating. In this story, Jesus is criticized for allowing his disciples to eat plucked grain on the Sabbath. Plucking the grain is work and therefore puts them in violation of Sabbath law. Jesus responds to this criticism by reminding his detractors of what David did while fleeing from Saul (1 Sam. 21:1–6). Although there are differences between David's story and the episode at hand (Donahue and Harrington, 111), the reference to David serves to parallel Jesus and David. The implicit argument was a common Jewish technique in which one argues from "light to heavy" (*qal we chomer*). The logic is that if David could claim special authority, then how much more so could Jesus, a point Marks makes explicit in 12:35–37. This special authority extends to his interpretation of what is proper to do on the Sabbath (2:28). He reminds them that the Sabbath was created to serve humans, not the other way around, a notion not foreign to Judaism (Hooker, 104; Juel, 54). This interpretation represents Jesus' basic view of the law—it is to help people, not hurt them.

In the middle of this section is the third episode (2:18–22), which illumines the surrounding stories. In response to questions raised about his disciples' lack of fasting, Jesus compares himself to a bridegroom. A wedding is a time of celebration, not of fasting. In the same manner, his disciples do not fast while he is with them. There will be time to fast when he is no longer there. Right now, a new thing is transpiring. It is symbolized by the images of wine, wineskins, and cloth, highlighting the two very different applications of the faith of Mark's day. The new wine and the new cloth of Jesus cannot fit within the current tradition. If the old does not change, it will cause the two to tear apart. By using the word *schisma* ("tear"), Mark calls his audience's attention back to Jesus' baptism, in which he uses the verbal form of *schisma* to describe the irreparable tearing of the heavens. Mark suggests that just as God ripped through the heavens to destroy the boundary between the Creator and creation, so God will rip through the current religious practices and traditions to destroy the social and economic systems that separate God's people from their God.

This tearing away emphasizes both the severity of the growing conflict between Jesus and the religious leaders and the intensity of the religious leaders' commitment to the prevailing social structure. With each successive story, more people are involved in the conflict. It starts with the scribes, who functioned as low-level officials and religious leaders invested with the authority to interpret Scripture. The Pharisees, who represented perhaps the most influential leadership group among the common people, show up next. It ends with the Pharisees and Herodians, most likely the courtiers of Herod, joining forces to kill Jesus (3:6). Moreover, as Jesus' opponents increase, so has the level of animosity against him. It begins with the scribes questioning in their hearts (2:6) and ends with a conspiracy to assassinate

Jesus (3:6). Jesus' response to his challengers also intensifies. He begins by merely responding to their questions and ends with outright anger (5:5), showing that his commitment to change the status quo is just as profound as the religious leaders' opposition.

The Text in the Interpretive Tradition

"Son of man" (*ho huios tou anthrōpou*), first mentioned in Mark 2:10, is the Greek translation of the Aramaic phrase *bar nasha*. The earliest commentators saw the son of man as a reference to the humanity of Jesus as it related to his earthly parentage. In the writings of Tertullian and Ignatius, both qualified "son of man" with the phrase "according to the flesh" to highlight Jesus' humanity and juxtaposed it to "Son of God," which highlighted his divinity. The early church fathers followed the Jewish understanding of the Hebrew form (*ben 'adam*), which refers to humanity in general. Within its Jewish context, "son of man" was believed to highlight the weakness and frailty of humanity. This is where the early church fathers' understanding of son of man differed from the Jewish understanding. For them, Jesus' divinity could in no way be compromised by human weakness.

The understanding of "son of man" as an affirmation of and emphasis on Jesus' humanity continued through the 1600s. However, new theories emerged after the Protestant Reformation. The two most predominant were from scholars who asserted that son of man was a messianic title based on Dan. 7:13 and those that argued that it was simply a self-reference. The understanding of "son of man" as a messianic title gained ground during the 1700s and 1800s. Yet the stress on Jesus' humanity remained. "Son of man" referred to a very human Messiah.

By the mid-1800s, this changed when an Ethiopic manuscript of *1 Enoch* was discovered that mentioned a preexistent heavenly son of man. For nearly a century, scholars asserted that Jesus' use of the phrase was based on this figure (France). During this same time period, scholars posited various theories: namely, that Jesus identified himself with the son of man that he expected to arrive during his lifetime (Joachim Jeremias); that the son of man was an allusion to and Jesus' acceptance of his role as an obedient servant (Morna Hooker); that the phrase was a creation of the early church; and that "son of man" was an idiom meaning "I," and therefore a nontitular self-reference (Géza Vermes). Scholarship remains divided on the theological interpretation of this phrase and whether it should be understood as a title or a simple self-designation. The lack of scholarly consensus has caused son of man studies to be described as "a prime illustration of the limits of New Testament scholarship" (Burkett, 5).

The Text in Contemporary Discussion

Scholars identify three types of son of man sayings in the Synoptic Gospels. They refer to (1) Jesus' earthly ministry, (2) his suffering, or (3) his future glory. The initial two son of man sayings in Mark's Gospel (2:10, 28) are located within the controversy cycles and refer to Jesus' earthly ministry. At the heart of the conflict are the boundary-breaking actions of Jesus that upset the social structure of his day. Interestingly enough, twenty-first-century American life reflects this aspect of Mark's world, a world in which 1 to 2 percent of the population controlled the vast majority of resources, leaving the rest barely able to survive (Saldarini, 40–41). We also live in a time and place in which scriptural interpretation and theological perspectives are used to support public policies and practices that deny people equal access under the law and basic forms of societal maintenance. Although we do not use the language of "unclean" to exclude people, we hear the labels "lazy," "deviant," and "dangerous" used to suggest that certain people are undeserving and unworthy of medical care, decent food and housing, equal rights under the law, or quality education because they are morally unfit or unqualified to reap societal benefits. Therefore, the ministry of the son of man in the controversy cycles poses questions to us: Who benefits from our interpretations of Scripture and practices of the faith? Who is excluded?

Mark 3:7–35

Following in Ministry: Expansion and Opposition

The Text in Its Ancient Context

Just as Mark recounted the upsurge of Jesus' fame due to the testimony of the leper (1:45), followed by the rise of opposition (2:1–3:6), so the pattern now continues. The crowds from Galilee are joined by those from Judea, Jerusalem, Idumea, beyond the Jordan (Perea), and the area of Tyre and Sidon. Although mentioned cursorily, the expansion of Jesus' following by people in these locales is significant in that it foreshadows the continued antagonism toward Jesus.

Initially of note is the fact that Mark mentions Judea and Jerusalem separately. At this time, the area that had long ago been the kingdoms of Israel and Judah comprised three regions: Judea, Samaria, and Galilee. Jerusalem was located in the region of Judea. However, Mark highlights the fact that people came not only from the smaller Judean towns and villages but also from the urban religious and political center of Jerusalem, the residence and spiritual base of the upper echelon of the Jewish religious leaders. It was also the political domain of the Roman procurator Pontius Pilate and the Roman client king Herod Antipas.

The inclusion of Idumea and Perea ("beyond the Jordan") as key places from which the multitudes have come gives further reason for the Herodians' animosity (3:6). The Herodians were most likely servants, courtiers, and/or officials of Herod. As supporters of Herod's rule, the Herodians would have found Jesus' preaching of a coming kingdom and (if known) his connection to the Davidic royal line to be a threat to their political interests (Meier, 744). At this point in the narrative, Jesus' ministry has been exclusively within the region of Galilee. Both Galilee and Perea were the original provinces given to Herod Antipas by Rome upon the death of his father, Herod the Great. Moreover, Idumea is the ancestral home of the Herodian dynasty.

Joining the people from Galilee, Judea, Jerusalem, Idumea, and Perea are the crowds that come from the area around Tyre and Sidon.

Jesus' ministry has now attracted gentiles from two of the leading Phoenician maritime merchant provinces of Rome. Their inclusion suggests that at some point, Jesus will also find himself in conflict with Rome.

The crowd has now swelled to "crushing" proportions. Despite the potentially deadly repercussions, Jesus does not scale back ministry but expands it. He calls twelve people to "be with him" and participate in ministry by preaching his kingdom message and having the authority to exorcize unclean spirits (3:14–15). Again, opposition will follow expansion. One of the twelve whom Jesus has chosen, Judas Iscariot, will betray him (3:19).

The pattern continues into the final portion of this section. Again, Mark notes the size of the crowd (3:20). What follows is a Markan inclusio—one story "sandwiched" between the beginning and end of another story—that highlights the opposition. The first conflict comes from an unexpected place, Jesus' own family. They believe that he is no longer in his right mind and are on their way to get him. Mark then turns the narrative lens to the "scribes from Jerusalem" who accuse Jesus of demon possession. They attribute his power to Beelzebul, the prince of demons. The story shifts back to Jesus' being told that his family is looking for him. Jesus redefines his family as those who "do the will of God" (3:35), which is precisely how Mark has depicted Jesus' ministry. Howard Clark Kee argues that this new eschatological family is a break from the actual family unit that allows followers of Jesus to form a new kinship group. It represents Markan "eschatological existence," which "involves the acceptance of present opportunities and obligations in view of the age to come" (Kee, 109).

The opposition to Jesus has arisen from every possible vantage point. He is confronted by his family and will soon face betrayal from one of his handpicked apostles. The spread of his fame and the increasing number of people drawn to him potentially threaten to exacerbate the tensions between him, the religious leaders in Jerusalem, and the supporters of Herod. Eventually, Jesus' ministry will catch the attention of Rome.

The Text in the Interpretive Tradition

One of the initial concerns for Roman Catholic interpreters of Mark 3:31–35 was reconciling the presence of Jesus' siblings (also mentioned in 6:3) and the perpetual virginity of Mary. Bede states emphatically, "the brothers of the Lord must not be thought to be the sons of the ever-virgin Mary." Jerome in his treatise *Against Helvidius* argues that Jesus' brothers were actually his cousins. Another argument for the perpetual virginity of Mary asserts that the siblings of Jesus were the children of Joseph from a previous marriage. However, the majority of scholars from the patristic period to the present focus on the formation of Jesus' new family.

John Chrysostom and John Calvin believed Jesus' actions demonstrated the primacy of spiritual relations over fleshly ones. Pseudo-Jerome held that these spiritual relations were not limited by gender. The inclusion of "sisters" in Jesus' new family (Mark 3:35) causes him to conclude: "He [Jesus] discerns us not by sex but by our deeds." Donald Juel avoids spiritualizing Jesus' words. Instead, he points out the controversial nature of denying the most basic social institution of the time, the family, and forging a new one (Juel, 65). Ched Myers articulates the eschatological role of Jesus' new family: it will socialize people into the kingdom just as the natural family socializes individuals into society (Myers, 168).

The Text in Contemporary Discussion

The phrase "family values" hit the national political scene in 1976, when the Republican Party decried the "erosion of family structures and family values." At the 1992 Republican National Convention, Pat Robertson and Dan Quayle claimed that "family values" were what the Republican Party stood for. Since then, the GOP has been criticized for its narrow definition of "family," often specified as a mother, a father, and their child/ren, when only 20 percent of US households fit this particular model. The phrase "family values" often works as code to refer to policies opposing reproductive and homosexual rights. But as historian Lawrence Stone observed while delivering the Tanner Lectures on Human Values at Harvard University, family values actually include several wider areas of social life: how children are socialized to fit into definitions of societal and individual roles, and a range of values concerning work, the accumulation of goods, sexual behavior, religion, and race (Stone, 70). In practice, any political party's policies will affect people's lives in all these areas.

In Mark 3:31–35, Jesus redefines his family. How might Mark's story of Jesus shape our behavior and affect our attitudes in terms of "family values," that is, our attitudes toward and behaviors concerning the areas just named?

Mark 4:1–34

Parables of the Kingdom

The Text in Its Ancient Context

Chapter 4 opens with the first discourse found in Mark. It contains three parables that use the common images of Galilean agrarian life: seeds and sowers. Jesus uses the parables to explain the kingdom he proclaims. The parables also serve to explain the rejection of Jesus and his kingdom message to Mark's readers.

The first parable describes a sower whose seed falls on four types of soil: a path, thorny ground, rocky ground, and good ground. The sower initially appears to be carelessly scattering seed. He has not identified a particular plot or portion of land to sow; nor is he careful about seed placement. Consequently, the majority of the parable is dedicated to describing the consequences: the seed does not grow from bad soil. However, the good soil produces an unimaginable harvest of thirty, sixty, and a hundredfold. These numbers vastly exceeded the 10 percent increase that a farmer would have considered a "bumper crop." Yet, no explanation is given about why the good soil produces such an unheard-of harvest. The assumption of the parable is that the seed is inherently good and only needs the right or good soil to produce copiously.

Producing a harvest at the level Jesus describes would have been a life-changing event for the masses that listened to him. Those gathered were more than likely dispossessed landowners or day laborers whose lack of employment and/or land enabled them to wander the countryside following Jesus (St. Clair, 105). They were ensnared by debt for their entire lives. The burden of Roman taxes, Jerusalem tithes, and the money required to seed the land and take care of a family left many people living at a subsistence level. The result is that those who had land often lost it because of debt. Those living on the land as tenant farmers could never earn enough to buy the land they worked. However, a harvest of thirty, sixty, or a hundredfold meant not only the difference between life and death but also freedom from a debt system that kept them in financial slavery (Myers, 177).

Although Jesus admonishes the crowd to listen, not everyone understands what he is saying. When the crowds have dispersed, those "around him" ask him to explain the parable. Before giving the explanation, he tells them that what they are in receipt of is the "mystery of the kingdom of God" (v. 11). Something is about to be revealed to them that will remain in parables to those "outside." This mystery is a dividing line that demarcates outsiders and insiders.

Mark's Jesus stresses the insider-outsider distinction by quoting Isa. 6:9–10. Whether the lack of understanding and subsequent repentance is the product of Jesus' intention or the consequence of one's failure to hear and accept Jesus' words depends on one's interpretation of *hina* in the Isa. 6:9–10 quotation as either an expression of purpose ("so that") or of result ("in order that"). Although C. S. Mann argues that determinism is a characteristic of apocalyptic and that an interpretation of purpose would not be surprising to Mark's audience, the subsequent parable in this chapter suggests a reading that implies *consequence*. Mark asserts that the meaning of Jesus' parable is "to be disclosed" and "come to light" (4:22). In addition, Mark will show the repeated misunderstanding of the Twelve, who are recipients of the parable's explanation.

Originally cast as insiders, their misunderstanding suggests a refusal on their part to heed what they have been taught. Thus the line Mark draws is traversable. Insiders could be "anyone" who has "ears to hear" and listen (v. 9). These receive the mystery of the kingdom that Jesus is giving to them. However, a refusal to hear and listen can relegate one to the outside.

What follows is an explanation of the parable that is critical for understanding all of the parables in Mark (v. 13). It begins simply: "The sower sows the word" (v. 14). The primary sower in Mark's Gospel is Jesus, whose ministry began with proclaiming the good news of God. His sowing, too, seems wasteful. The vast majority of those who gather around him when he is giving the word are poor, diseased, demon-possessed, or considered sinners. They lack economic means and social acceptance and cannot attain the standards of ritual purity. Although their lack relegates them to the margins of their current society, it will not hinder their participation or production in the kingdom of God. According to the parable, Satan, persecution or trouble, and wealth or worldly desires cause spiritual barrenness. But if people will hear, accept, and act on the word, then they, too, can be fruitful (v. 20).

In short, the kingdom is not what people would expect. It is hidden (vv. 22) like a seed on the earth that is not readily seen but takes time to grow and make its presence known (vv. 26–29). It starts small and looks insignificant but becomes great (vv. 30–32). One could easily dismiss the kingdom and its messenger. For this reason, Jesus admonishes those around him (and Mark, by extension, is telling his readers) to "listen" (v. 22) and "pay attention" (v. 23), lest they too become the bad soil that rejects the seed of this sower.

The Text in the Interpretive Tradition

The earliest interpretations of Jesus' parables were allegorical in nature. The early church read parables as stories that used earthly symbols to communicate heavenly truths. Pseudo-Jerome wrote that Jesus spoke in parables so that "those who could not take in heavenly things, might conceive what they heard by an earthly similitude." The first major departure from an allegoristic approach was by Adolf Jülicher in 1888. He argued that Jesus would not have used coded language; therefore, the allegorical interpretations of the parables were the creation of the Gospel writers. Interestingly enough, the patristic and medieval interpreters had no problem with the coded language of the parables. Although they believed the ability to see or understand was a result of God's grace, the lack of understanding was attributed to human unwillingness (Pseudo-Chrysostom), specifically people "mak[ing] themselves not to see" (Theophylact).

Scholars who followed in the wake of Jülicher, like Joachim Jeremias, believed that by studying the parables one could reconstruct the situation in which they developed and uncover the original sayings of Jesus. The next shift occurred when the focus of study moved from the world behind the text to the narrative world of the text. Contemporary scholars now look at the literary context of the parables to ascertain their meaning and seek to be mindful of the insider-outsider dynamic of the text by acknowledging both the comfort and the discomfort created by the text.

The Text in Contemporary Discussion

Parables are tricky. One the one hand, they use familiar imagery to communicate a message. This lends an air of accessibility; it makes one feel like the parables can be easily understood. Yet this is not the case for those around Jesus in Mark's Gospel. He must explain the parables, and then only does so in private, thereby erecting a wall between those on the inside, who understand, and those on the outside, who do not. Coded language separates, and the inevitability of its separating function is often uncomfortable. The first major interpretive shift in the study of parables occurred precisely because of a scholar's discomfort with Jesus' use of coded language. Yet some people are comfortable with coded language. They see the boundaries that the code erects as necessary for survival and communication. The apocalyptic language of

Daniel and Revelation and the use of spirituals by African Americans are two examples.

Mark 4:35–6:6

Ministry and Rejection

The Text in Its Ancient Context

Writing shortly after the fall of the Jerusalem temple, Mark responds to the religious crisis by encouraging his readers to follow Jesus. In this section, Mark makes it clear to the Jews and gentiles that constitute his audience that following Jesus will require the inclusion of the gentiles as well as Jews like the woman with the hemorrhage, who have found themselves marginalized by Jewish law.

After a day of public and private instruction on the kingdom of God, Jesus decides to take his disciples to the "other side" of the lake (4:35). Before they reach gentile soil, however, a storm arises that threatens to keep them from reaching their destination. It also causes the disciples to fear for their lives (4:38). Within the narrative context, the storm could be symbolic of the Jewish attitudes that oppose the inclusion of the gentiles. Since Jesus is able to subdue nature in the same way he has been able to subdue demons, the disciples do not perish as they follow Jesus' command to cross over. Mark, therefore, shows his readers that this ministerial direction is by divine proclamation and under divine protection.

According to Mark, Jesus and his disciples disembark in the land of the Gerasenes (5:1). Although the name of this region differs from that given in Matthew (Gadarenes, 8:28) and its location is unknown, it is a gentile territory near the Decapolis, a group of ten Greek city-states southeast of the Sea of Galilee. This area represents the height of uncleanness for Jews. The first person Jesus and the disciples encounter is a man possessed by so many demons that they refer to themselves as "Legion" (5:9). He lives among the tombs, a place inhabited by the dead (5:3). There is a "great herd" of pigs nearby (5:11).

It seems that Jesus has entered the "strong man's house" (3:27) by invading enemy territory both spiritually and politically. "Legion" is the name of a Roman military unit composed of about six thousand soldiers. During this time, the soldiers stationed in Palestine displayed a wild boar as their symbol. Although the demons possess the man, their control of him is secondary to their desire to remain within that particular geographical locale. After begging Jesus not to send them out of the region (*chora*, 5:10), they beg him to send them into the swine (5:12). By exorcizing the demons, Jesus has "plundered [the strong man's] property" (3:27). He is strong enough to subdue the demoniac (5:4) because he is the stronger one whom John foretold (1:7). Mark shows his readers that this foray into gentile territory does not result in the demise of Jesus or his disciples. Neither does it contaminate them. On the contrary, it results in the drowning of the demon-possessed pigs in the sea, like Pharaoh's army in Exodus, and produces another disciple who follows Jesus in his preaching ministry (5:20).

Next, Jesus and his disciples return to Jewish soil. Mark now links the stories of Jairus's daughter and the woman with the issue of blood. Both are referred to as "daughter" (5:23, 34), a familial designation that suggests they are part of the Jewish community. Given that the number twelve, the number of Israel's tribes, is used with reference to both women, perhaps Mark intends these two females to symbolize Israel.

This passage begins with Jairus's begging Jesus to heal his daughter. If the two women are meant to represent Judaism in some way, then Jairus's daughter might represent Jews whose lives are properly circumscribed by the law. The little girl is the legitimate offspring of her father (5:23). He speaks on her behalf and solicits the aid she needs. Moreover, he is a leader of a synagogue. He and his family would have been fully included in the community. Furthermore, her age suggests that she is still virginal. Her presence within the home suggests that she is ritually clean. However, none of this prevents her from being sick to the point of death and needing Jesus to heal her.

Before the girl is healed, Jesus is stopped by the touch of a woman who has suffered from hemorrhages for twelve years. She may represent those who have been marginalized by the law. Her condition renders her status as perpetually ritually unclean (Leviticus 15), and she has found no one to help her. Like the little girl, she is sick. She has gone to physicians, but the physicians have not made her better. She too needs Jesus in order to be healed. However, her healing will restore more than her health. It will restore her place within the community. She will no longer be excluded by virtue of her disease.

Critical to each story is Jesus. If these women are meant to represent classes of people, Mark may be showing that Jesus' ministry is needed not only for the gentiles to be delivered (5:1–20) but also for Israel to be healed. By placing the little girl's healing last, perhaps Mark suggests that Israel will not be healed until not only the gentiles but also the Jews who have been marginalized by the law are included. Like the father who was told to "only believe" (5:36) and the woman whose "faith made [her] well" (5:34), Israel must heed Jesus' kingdom message and believe the good news.

Unfortunately, the prospect of this occurring does not look good. Earlier, the gentiles begged Jesus to leave their neighborhood (5:17). Now, although a crowd is pressing in on Jesus, only one person has enough faith to get Jesus' attention (5:30–31). Rather than celebrate the fact that the little girl is not dead, the mourners laugh at Jesus (5:40). Even the people from Jesus' hometown are offended (*skandalizein*) by him (6:3). Their unbelief amazes Jesus (6:6). Yet the only scandalous thing Mark has shown Jesus do is minister to those who have been left out.

The Text in the Interpretive Tradition

This section contains four of the most extraordinary miracles in the Gospel. During the late nineteenth and early twentieth centuries, scholars from the history of religions school began to explore the Hellenistic origins of Christianity. In 1935, Ludwig Bieler published a two-volume work, *Theios Anēr*, which cataloged the characteristics of the Greek "divine man" (*theios anēr*) and listed examples of the divine man in ancient literature including the Bible. One of the characteristics of the divine man was the performance of miracles. Based on the similarities discovered between Hellenistic figures and Jesus, a *theios anēr* or god-man Christology arose. Redaction critics who accepted the existence of a *theios anēr* Christology argued that Mark was written as either a modification of it (Keck) or an outright rejection of it (Weeden). Other scholars, such as Barry Blackburn, deny a *theios anēr* Christology in Mark and argue that the miracle stories are derived from a Jewish rather than a Hellenistic context. Narrative critics, on the other hand, were not concerned about the miracle stories' connection to a cultural milieu. Instead, they looked at how these stories moved Mark's plot forward and attended to the expansion of Jesus' ministry and mission.

The Text in Contemporary Discussion

On January 20, 2009, Barack Hussein Obama was inaugurated as the forty-fourth president of the United States of America. He was the first African American to hold this nation's highest political office. This led many to conclude that the United States was now a "post-racial" society. Somehow President Obama's election was believed to be the death knell of racism, race-based discrimination, and prejudice. It proved that America was whole, or at the very least no longer divided by race. Yet Sunday mornings remain the most segregated time of the American day, and church pews remain one of the most segregated places.

At the time of President Obama's election, approximately 5 percent of US churches were racially integrated or had 20 percent or more of their members represent a different racial/ethnic background from the majority group. Half of these congregations were trending toward a single ethnic identity, which was a reflection of the basic preference among all racial groups: homogeneity. In order for a congregation to be truly multicultural, no single racial identity can dominate its religious life or practice. This means that more than the face of the congregation must change. The congregation must be prepared for changes in things like leadership, worship practices, mission projects, and financial priorities.

As we reflect on this passage in Mark, it is important for us to consider honestly who the gentiles would be to us—whose racial/ethnic background is not only different from our own but also what separates us from each other. Who would be the outcasts—the people who share a similar racial/ethnic background but whose social, cultural, and/or economic status separates us from them? What storms could potentially arise if we were to "cross over to the other side"? Would our declining and dying congregations be resurrected if we, too, included the modern-day equivalent to Mark's "outsider" (gentile) and "outcast"? What would national policies like immigration, health-care reform, and welfare reform look like?

Mark 6:7–29

Ministry and Murder

The Text in Its Ancient Context

Whereas the parable of the sower in chapter 4 focuses on the condition of the soil (4:3–8), this section reveals the possible consequences of sowing the word. The theme began with the sending out of the Twelve whom Jesus called to be with him, proclaim the message, and have authority over unclean spirits (3:14–15). This is the same ministry work that Mark records Jesus doing and that the disciples now perform (6:12–13). Jesus gives them specific instructions on how to govern themselves and what to bring with them. It is clear that Jesus expects the people to welcome the itinerant ministers because he tells them to take nothing with them except a staff (6:8). The *Didache* also shares this expectation of hospitality (*Did.* 11.1–12). However, Jesus is aware that not everyone will receive the Twelve. In this instance, they are to shake the dust from their feet (6:11), thereby disassociating themselves from the bad soil that does not listen and accept the word.

The ministry of the Twelve is apparently successful. People begin to speculate that John the Baptist or Elijah has been raised from the dead (6:14–15). The ministry work of the disciples, work that clearly mirrors the ministry of Jesus, is now connected to John the Baptist. Prior to this point, Mark has told the reader that John was arrested (1:14). Now the reader finds out that John has been beheaded by Herod (6:16) and his death was orchestrated by Herodias (6:19–24). Like Jezebel, who sought to kill Elijah for condemning the worship of her gods and killing her prophets (1 Kings 19:1–2), Herodias wanted John executed for speaking against her marriage to Herod (6:18–19).

At this point in the narrative, one sower is dead, and sowing the word lies at the root of his death. Members of Mark's community, who already know of Jesus' death, would also know that John will not be the only casualty in Mark's story. Jesus will die, and Mark is laying the foundation to connect his death to John's. In Mark's narrative, both men are "handed over" or "betrayed" (*paradothēnai*, 1:14; 3:19; 14:41). The means of death (beheading and crucifixion) are the most shameful ways of executing a person during this time. Mark shows their words to be the precipitating factor in their deaths (6:18; 14:62). The people's assertion that John has been raised from the dead (6:14) prepares Mark's audience for Jesus' prediction of his own resurrection (8:31; 9:31; 10:34).

Upon the disciples' return, Jesus decides that they should get away from the crowds and rest (6:31). However, they cannot escape the multitudes. The people flock to where they are. The scene is reminiscent of Israel in the wilderness, whose hunger is satisfied by manna, bread from heaven. In this instance, Jesus looks up to heaven, blesses and breaks five loaves, divides two fish, and gives them to his disciples to distribute (6:41). At least five thousand people are fed (6:44). Once again, Jesus and his disciples are aligned in ministry. Yet Mark will show that they still do not grasp the significance of who Jesus is, and therefore cannot possibly understand the consequences of following in a ministry like his.

The Text in the Interpretive Tradition

In 1901, Wilhelm Wrede published his groundbreaking work, *Das Messiasgeheimnis in den Evangelien*. He is credited with being "the first to appreciate the theological nature of the synoptics" (Dunn, 92). His basic thesis was that Jesus' silencing of demons, healed persons, Peter after his confession at Caesarea Philippi, and the disciples after the transfiguration as well as the private instruction, parabolic teachings, and continued misunderstanding of the disciples (like the misunderstanding about the loaves in 6:52 noted above) are all a part of the "messianic secret." The messianic secret was Mark's attempt to resolve the tension between the early church's claim that Jesus is the Messiah and Jesus' not claiming this role for himself in the Gospel. Wrede believed that the messianic secret was not historical in origin, but rather a theological motif created by and imposed on the Gospel by Mark.

James Blevins traces three waves of reactions during the first seventy years after the release of Wrede's monograph. The first decade was characterized by a widespread rejection of his theory. The few who accepted it did so in modified form. For example, Albert Schweitzer accepted Wrede's theory but did not attribute the secrecy theme to Mark. Modifications of the theory continued into the next wave of reactions. During the second and third decades, scholars tried to connect the motif to the historical Jesus. Form critics who accepted Wrede's argument noted that certain elements included in the secrecy motif, like the silencing of demons, was not the work of Mark, but preredaction material. During the years just before and after World War II (fourth and fifth decades), a primary issue was whether the secrecy motif originated with Jesus, and was therefore historical in nature, or with Mark, thereby making the Gospel a wholly theological construction.

This interplay between history and theology also emerges in this section, when Mark lays the death of John the Baptist at the feet of Herodias (Mark 6:19, 24; cf. Matt. 14:8). Mark portrays Herod as easily manipulated and an unwilling partner in Herodias's deadly scheme. However, Josephus attributes John's death to Herod's fear of John's popularity (*Ant.* 18.116–19), not Herodias's "grudge against him" (6:19). According to Bede, it is not Herod's fear but Herodias's fear of Herod repenting of his marriage to her that is the impetus for her murderous designs. Theophylact also implied Herodias's culpability by claiming that lust is what prompted Herod to comply with his wife's wishes. Despite Josephus's assertion and the Herodian rulers' hunger for political power, both biblical scholarship and popular culture have left Herodias's diabolical role in John's death unquestioned.

In medieval Europe, Herodias was said to fly through the night once a year and was purported to be the leader of a cult of witches. During the nineteenth century, Flaubert and Massanet both wrote stories in which Herodias bore all the features of a stereotypical femme fatale. Contemporary Mark scholars pay little attention to the historical Herodias. Their focus tends to be more theological as they note the similarities between John's and Jesus' death, the analogous roles Herod and Pilate played in their respective deaths, and the parallels between John, Herod, and Herodias and Elijah, Ahab, and Jezebel.

The Text in Contemporary Discussion

Although much of Wrede's thesis has been dismissed or modified by subsequent scholars, any discussion of Mark's Gospel must take it into consideration. C. S. Mann correctly asserts, "The 'secrecy' motif is too strongly entrenched in the narrative to be dismissed lightly" (Mann, 216). However, it is almost universally agreed that Wrede's "messianic secrecy" is too limiting a category to house such "disparate phenomena" (Donahue and Harrington, 28) that have a "variety of motives" at work (Dunn, 98). Since the World War II years, scholarship remains divided on whether the secrecy motif finds its genesis in Jesus or Mark. On one end of the debate are those who locate the motif's origin with Jesus, who was afraid that revealing himself would incite a military revolt. On the other end are those who say it is a creation of Mark, who seeks thereby to explain why Jesus does not claim to be the Messiah in his Gospel. At the heart of the issue is whether the origin of Mark's Gospel is historical or theological.

Meanwhile, the work of feminists, which has drawn scholarly attention to the negative portrayal of Herodias, struggles with the historical and theological interplay in Scripture. They admonish readers of the biblical text to beware when reading stories about women because historically these have been "stories by men about women" (Schüssler Fiorenza, 50). They reveal the patriarchal language in the text in which

Herodias is referred to as a possession belonging to Herod's brother (6:18). They call attention to the contradiction between Herodias's alleged power in having John killed and her absence from Herod's birthday celebration, which suggests she was not important enough to attend. They examine the roles of women within the sociocultural world that shaped the Gospels. This allows them to show how women have been misrepresented, overlooked, or even vilified.

Narrative readings allow scholars to hold the story world of Mark together with its theological import while examining the historical background of the text. Narrative critics see Mark as an author with an important story to tell. In the case of Herodias, narrative critics look at how a woman has been characterized: What does the author show and tell us about her? Does she espouse or reject the evaluative point of view (the belief system or moral disposition) of the narrator? What are her character traits? If the portrayal in Mark's Gospel is negative, it is also important to ask if her role is consistent with Mark's characterization of other women his Gospel, or does he present a variety of female characters? While her story as presented by Mark may not be historically accurate, it can help the reader understand Mark's story better.

Mark 7:1–23

Ministry and Tradition

The Text in Its Ancient Context

Jesus' popularity among the masses has gotten the attention of the religious leaders in Jerusalem (7:1). Previously, the scribes who had come from Jerusalem accused Jesus of being possessed by Beelzebul (3:22). Now the Pharisees join the scribes. The point of contention is the "tradition of the elders," the oral law that was eventually written in the Mishnah, as it relates to hand washing. The scribes and Pharisees notice that Jesus' disciples do not wash their hands before eating, and question why (7:2, 5). At the root of their concern is more than hand washing; it is the practice of their faith.

Whereas Mark's response to post-temple Judaism is to encourage following Jesus, the Pharisees' response was to bring holiness into everyday life. In their opinion, Jews could uphold God's requirement for holiness (Lev. 11:44, 45; 19:2) by ordering life in such a way that all they did and touched was sanctified. This required avoiding anything that defiled a person. To disregard the practices that helped to cleanse daily life was to dismantle the faith and disregard the oral tradition. This dismantling was, in their eyes, as destructive to Judaism as was the destruction of the temple. For the Pharisee, on the one hand, the Torah as interpreted by the oral tradition mediated the relationship between God and God's people. Mark, on the other hand, sees Jesus fulfilling that role (Juel, 106–7).

According to Mark, Jesus asserts that "human tradition" and the commands of God are at variance with one another (7:8–9). At the heart of Jesus' concern is the inclusion of those heretofore excluded from the practice of the faith. When Mark writes that "all the Jews" do not eat with unwashed hands (7:3), he is using "Jews" to refer to those who adhered to the teachings of Pharisaic Judaism because he has not shown this to be the practice of the Jewish followers of Jesus. It would have been virtually impossible for the five thousand men fed in the wilderness to have washed their hands before eating (6:44). Neither does he record any hand washing before the meal at Levi's house (2:15). Moreover, it is doubtful that many of the people who came to Jesus would have been concerned with, or had the means of maintaining vigilant hand-washing practices, since these persons were predominantly indigent, ill, or demon-possessed. Consequently, Mark's use of "all of the Jews" is inaccurate. However, saying "all the Jews" allows him to separate the practices of his community not only from Pharisaic Judaism but also Judaism in general. Therefore, Jesus' refusal to uphold the tradition of hand washing is no longer a difference of opinion with those from a particular branch of Judaism but represents a rift with Judaism itself. It also allows gentiles and Jews who do not or cannot keep the traditions of the elders to follow Jesus.

Jesus begins his critique of the tradition by quoting Isa. 29:13. He uses the words of the prophet to argue against the practices of the

Pharisees. In short, they are hypocritical (7:6). Their tradition actually militates against true worship of God (7:7). Consequently, the Jews in Mark's community need not feel obligated to follow the Pharisees or feel excluded by them. Moreover, the gentiles in Mark's community can reach the same conclusion, as it is clear that Mark is writing to them also. He explains what "defiled hands" mean (7:2), expounds on the "tradition of elders" (7:3–4), and translates the Aramaic word *korban* (7:11).

Jesus pushes his kingdom agenda further by using this opportunity to explain what truly defiles a person. Mark refers to Jesus' teaching here as a "parable" (7:17). As with the telling of the parables in chapter 4, Jesus commands those around him to "listen" (7:14). Moreover, he explains the meaning of the parable to his disciples in private. These similarities intimate that Jesus is telling his listeners something about the kingdom of God.

Specifically, Jesus teaches that an understanding of defilement in terms of the kingdom of God is not about what goes in but what goes out (7:15, 20). There is a difference between the stomach and the heart (7:19). What comes out of the heart corrupts. What goes in the stomach does not have the power to defile, leaving Mark to conclude that Jesus has "declared all foods clean" (7:19). How one eats (whether the hands are washed or unwashed) and what one eats (whether the food is deemed clean or unclean according to dietary laws) no longer has the power to deny persons a relationship with God or prevent participation among the people of God.

The Text in the Interpretive Tradition

Readings of this passage have primarily focused on the dispute between Jesus and the Pharisees over the validity of oral law. Many commentators equated "oral law" with "man-made" law because they were unaware that the Pharisees believed in a dual Torah, written and oral, that was revealed to Moses on Sinai (Donahue and Harrington, 228). However, interpretations became more nuanced as scholars began to examine the

Jewish context of Jesus' ministry and no longer to view first-century Judaism in monolithic terms. Instead, scholars began to see the varied strands of Judaism and how they responded to the fall of the Jerusalem temple. Consequently, descriptions of Pharisaic Judaism went beyond labels of "religious legalism." Attention to the sociocultural context of Mark's Gospel filled out the flat characters that Mark presented. It also prompted contemporary scholars to view this passage as breaking the barriers that would have prevented gentile participation in the early church. This passage clarified for Mark's community its stand on issues that would have distinguished it from Pharisaic Judaism.

The Text in Contemporary Discussion

In almost every religious tradition, there is a belief that certain things or people have the power to defile individuals or the community. There are usually two basic approaches to dealing with the pollutant: washing machine or garbage disposal. At the heart of the washing-machine approach is the conviction that the power to cleanse is greater than the power to contaminate. Therefore, the polluted thing or person can be cleaned up and restored to inclusion. When one opts for the garbage-disposal approach, there is a belief that the power to contaminate is greater than the power to cleanse. Consequently, the pollutant must be removed before it corrupts another individual or community. One's approach depends on the particular contaminant being addressed, and both approaches can be utilized within the same religious tradition. For example, unwashed hands, certain foods, and table fellowship with the wrong people were just a few of the contaminants that first-century Pharisees believed made a person unclean. Hands could be purified by washing (the washing-machine approach) and certain foods and people could be avoided (the garbage-disposal approach).

What are the pollutants that we fear in our contemporary practice of the faith? Which ones do we believe have a power to contaminate that is greater than the power to cleanse (requiring us to use a garbage-disposal approach)? Over what pollutants is the power to cleanse greater than the pollutants' power to defile (so we may use the washing-machine approach)? According to Mark, Jesus redefines what defiles a person and thereby pronounces all food clean (7:19). By so doing, he eradicates the need to employ either the washing-machine or the garbage-disposal models because there no longer exists any need for cleansing. Do we need to amend our understanding of what defiles and therefore our approach to some things and/or some people?

Mark 7:24–8:26

Receptivity and Misunderstanding

The Text in Its Ancient Context

Jesus again journeys into gentile territory. This trip reveals the receptivity of the gentiles to Jesus' ministry and proves that there is room for them to be included. Mark, then, uses the receptivity of the gentiles to highlight the growing lack of perceptivity of the Jews whom Jesus encounters throughout this section.

Jesus' first stop is in the region of Tyre. There, he meets a Syrophoenician woman who begs him to cast a demon out of her daughter (7:26). Initially, Jesus seems disinclined to help her. He dismisses her by insisting that "the children" (Israel) are to be fed (*chortasthēnai*) first (7:27). To do otherwise is tantamount to giving their food to dogs (7:28). Although Jesus calls her a dog (7:27), the woman is not dissuaded. She insists that even the dogs get crumbs (7:28). Jesus validates her statement by casting the demon out of her daughter (7:29–30). However, the veracity of her statement has farther-reaching implications than the fulfillment of an individual request.

By recounting the feeding of the five thousand in a manner that alluded to Israel's experience of manna in the wilderness, Mark had shown that "the children" have already eaten to the point of satisfaction (6:42). There he used the same verb that occurs in 7:27 (*chortasthēnai*) to convey that the desert meal filled them. He also noted that the disciples collected twelve baskets of leftovers, symbolically suggesting a basket from each of the twelve tribes of Israel. Indeed, there are crumbs from the children's table, and now Jesus meets a woman so hungry for his help that she is willing to receive these scraps. Mark further emphasizes the gentile woman's hunger for Jesus' ministry by placing her story immediately after Jesus' confrontation with the scribes and Pharisees. While the Pharisees and scribes were concerned with the purity of one's hands and one's food, the gentile woman is willing to eat off the floor to get what she needs from Jesus. By linking her story to the feeding of the five thousand and positioning it immediately after Jesus' argument with the scribes and Pharisees, Mark argues that the inclusion of gentiles will neither prevent nor lessen what God has for the Jews.

Upon leaving Tyre, Jesus travels to the region of the Decapolis. Mark identifies this place as the locale of the former demoniac's preaching ministry. It is here that he proclaimed what Jesus had done for him (5:20). Earlier, the people of this region begged Jesus to leave (5:17). Now they beg Jesus to heal a deaf and mute man (7:32). Jesus heals the man "in private, away from the crowd" (7:33) and forbids the people from telling it. Yet they proclaim it "zealously" (7:36), thereby joining the former demoniac in his preaching ministry by again proclaiming what Jesus has done.

The two preceding events occur at the initiative of gentiles. They seek out Jesus and request his aid. The feeding of the four thousand, which is the last act Mark records as occurring on gentile soil, happens at Jesus' initiative. Like the feeding of the five thousand on Jewish soil, the motivation behind this miracle is Jesus' compassion. However, Jesus had compassion for the Israelites because they lacked leaders (6:34). Here, Mark emphasizes the receptivity of the gentiles to Jesus' ministry by noting that the crowd has been with Jesus for three days (8:2). As a result, they are hungry. However, their physical hunger is the direct result of their hunger for Jesus, a hunger that causes them to remain with him for three days without food. Therefore, Jesus responds.

Using seven loaves and a few small fish, he feeds the four thousand gathered around him. Jesus has now used a total of twelve loaves to feed both Jews and gentiles. The number twelve may allude to the twelve tribes of Israel. If this is the case, then Mark is letting his community know that what has been given to Israel is more than enough to satisfy both groups. The supply is so great that neither group can exhaust it. Like the Jews who were fed in the wilderness, the gentiles are filled (*chortasthēnai*) and there are still leftovers (8:8).

After the feeding of the four thousand, Jesus immediately returns to Jewish territory. Here he is met with skepticism and misunderstanding. His first encounter is with Pharisees who demand a "sign from heaven" (8:11). Jesus refuses to oblige them (8:12). However, Mark has answered their question for the reader, with the details he has included in his Gospel. He has recounted the heavens opening (1:10), a voice from heaven at Jesus' baptism (1:11), Jesus looking to heaven as he blessed the five loaves he used to feed five thousand people (6:41), and Jesus looking up to heaven before healing the deaf mute (7:34). Although Mark never mentions the presence of the Pharisees at the aforementioned events, his narrative flow makes the Pharisees appear obtuse to the reader. Because Mark's audience has been given all these "signs from heaven," they are left to assume that the Pharisees should understand rather than argue.

Misunderstanding is not a quality reserved for Jesus' enemies alone. There is much his disciples do not get. Mark shows their lack of understanding in the next episode. Jesus warns them about the "yeast of the Pharisees" and the "yeast of Herod" (8:15). They do not grasp the symbolic use of yeast as a corrupting agent (Donahue and Harrington, 252). Instead, they think Jesus is talking about their lack of physical bread. Even if they could not appreciate the full intent of Jesus' warning, the fact that they think Jesus is troubled by a lack of bread after feeding at least nine thousand people with only twelve loaves shows their imperceptivity.

This section closes with Jesus' healing a blind man. What is unique about this account is that Jesus must lay his hands on the man twice to fully restore his sight (8:23, 25). Given Jesus' command of nature, authority over demons, ability to multiply fish and loaves, and healing virtue that is so strong that touching his garments restores people to full health, the need to touch the blind man twice does not suggest a diminishment of Jesus' power. Instead, it points to the persistent imperceptivity of the disciples. They are blind like this man. They do not get it on the first encounter. They see a little, but they do not yet grasp the whole thing.

The Text in the Interpretive Tradition

Some of the earliest commentators on the story of the Syrophoenician woman (7:24–30) focus on the woman as model of faithful persistence. Bede describes her reply to Jesus' initial refusal of her request as both "humble and faithful." He asserts that these are the qualities that garnered her request. Calvin observes, "she adhered firmly to . . . [her] sentiment of faith" despite the fact that Jesus "[makes] trial of her faith" (Calvin 1845, 2:266–68). Although he describes her actions as "presumptuous," most early commentators downplay her transgression of social boundaries by finding qualities such as humility and service in her behavior. Pseudo-Chrysostom goes so far as to say her reverence was demonstrated by placing herself at the level of a dog. Feminist and womanist scholars broke from this tradition by highlighting her disregard of social convention and applauding her bold behavior. They point to her "sass" (womanists) and her wit (feminists), rather than traditional female virtues of passivity and submission, as the reason she got what she needed from Jesus.

The Text in Contemporary Discussion

Scholars have attempted to soften the impact of Jesus' calling the Syrophoenician woman a "dog," by (1) drawing attention to more positive gentile understandings of "dog" as a house pet (!); (2) pointing out that Jesus actually referred to her and her child as "little dogs" (*kynaria*), which is less offensive than "dog" (*kyōn*); or (3) arguing that Jesus' words represented prevailing Jewish opinion about gentiles, rather than his own perception of the woman, in order to counter opposition to gentile inclusion. The fact remains, however, that this ethnic slur is found on the lips of Jesus.

Now consider how common it has become in some parts of popular culture today to refer to women in general, and African American women in particular, as "bitches" (female dogs). The lyrics of many hip-hop songs equate "bitch" with "woman." Reducing women to the level of animals allows men outright to exploit them or treat them as pets (Collins). Moreover, women are also referred to as "hoes" (whores), thereby relegating them to the status of sex objects, or as "chickenheads," persons of intellectual inferiority. Social theorists and feminist scholars acknowledge that while it is easy to point out the vulgar references to women in hip-hop and especially its subgenre gangsta rap, these are merely the blatant expression of a wider societal misogyny.

The attempts by Mark scholars to neutralize the "dog" language in the text is akin to the efforts of some women and that of some African Americans to defuse the racist and misogynistic import of the *b* and the *n* word. As people argue both sides of the issue, the question remains: Are there words that are so negative that it is impossible to redeem their meaning or their use? If so, what do we do with a text like Mark 7:24–30?

Mark 8:27–10:52

Following on the Way

The Text in Its Ancient Context

Jesus' lessons on discipleship and the misunderstanding of his disciples typify this section. Although Jesus' lessons have the disciples as their narrative audience, Mark shows that anyone can follow Jesus (Malbon 1986). Like Jesus' original disciples, however, many will misunderstand. Therefore, Mark employs Jesus' passion prediction and lessons to prepare a would-be disciple for both the call and consequences of discipleship (St. Clair 2008).

Discipleship is not for the fainthearted; no one finds it easy (Malbon 1983, 29). Defined primarily in terms of servanthood, discipleship runs counter to a social structure that advances persons with access to wealth, power, authority, and even purity to the highest levels of the social order. Those without access to this social currency remained at the lowest levels. Thus the way of Jesus reverses the honor-shame codes that structure the cultural world in which Mark's audience lives (St. Clair, 109–64).

Mark first attends to Jesus' identity. Peter declares Jesus to be the "Messiah" (*christos*, 8:27), and for the first time within the narrative, someone uses the same title as that found in the opening line of the Gospel (1:1). Jesus' response confirms the veracity of Peter's answer. He orders Peter and the disciples to keep silent for the same reason he forbade the demons to speak: they knew him (1:25, 34; 3:11).

On the heels of Peter's confession, Jesus foretells his suffering, death, and resurrection (8:31). Although Peter has correctly identified Jesus as the Christ, he does not fully grasp the consequences of Jesus' messianic ministry. He therefore attempts to silence Jesus by rebuking (*epitimān*, 8:32) him as Jesus has rebuked the demons. Rather than silencing Jesus, Peter's actions precipitate Jesus' first lesson on discipleship. Jesus teaches that following him will necessitate two things that run counter to the cultural values of ancient Mediterranean society. First, a would-be disciple must deny himself or herself (8:34). For Mark's original audience, self-denial meant leaving behind one's primary group affiliation (usually the family or kinship group) and solely identifying with Jesus and his gospel. The would-be disciple would need to do "the will of God" so that Jesus and his followers become his or her "brother and sister and mother" (3:35). She or he would then seek approval from Jesus rather than their original group or society at large (St. Clair, 135–36). Second, she or he must "take up the cross" (8:34). The cross represented the most painful and humiliating death that Rome could exact on its subjects. Therefore, Jesus' disciples needed to be able to face pain and shame as a result of following Jesus. In short, a follower of Jesus needed to be prepared to die (St. Clair, 138).

Six days later, Jesus takes Peter, James, and John up a high mountain, where he is transfigured in the presence of Moses and Elijah. Their presence with Jesus suggests that the law (Moses) and the prophets (Elijah) reach their fullest expression in Jesus. Their disappearance, leaving Jesus standing alone, suggests that Jesus has the final authoritative word.

Once again, Peter misunderstands. Whether he proposes the booths to prolong the mountaintop experience (Donahue and Harrington, 270) or he believes this event signals the time Zechariah foretold (14:12–21) in which the survivors of the war against Jerusalem would celebrate the Feast of Booths (Juel, 128), he knows he stands at a critical moment. However, the correct response is neither speaking nor building: he needs to listen.

Peter, however, is not the only one struggling to follow Jesus. The remaining nine disciples have also been having difficulty. They have been unable to cast a spirit out of a little boy (9:17). Before rebuking the spirit, Jesus criticizes those around him, including his disciples, for their lack of faith. Faithlessness both characterizes their generation (9:19) and reveals the disciples' lack of identification with Jesus and his words. They are more like the people around them than they are like Jesus.

Jesus must start from the beginning. He foretells his suffering and death for the second time (9:31). Rather than ask Jesus for clarification, the disciples argue about who is the greatest (9:34). Jesus' teaching again reverses the honor-shame codes: status comes through service (9:35). The one willing to humble oneself to the level of the least is the greatest. Jesus illustrates this point by taking a child, the person with the least social status, in his arms (9:36). If one can welcome such a person of low estate in Jesus' name, it will be like welcoming Jesus (9:32). Mark then highlights Jesus' lesson by presenting four episodes that deal with the treatment of the least.

The first episode concerns an exorcist who casts out demons using Jesus' name but does not follow Jesus like the disciples (9:38). For this reason, the disciples try to stop him. Jesus forbids them to stop him and warns them about putting a "stumbling block before one of these little ones" (9:42). "Little ones" are the followers of Jesus who are called to be the servant(s) of all (9:35). Though society may view them as small in social stature and having little power, the "little ones" are great in the kingdom. The sin of hindering their discipleship is so egregious that it is better to cut off the offending body parts rather than risk hellfire (9:43–47).

Jesus' description of the "little ones" as those who believe in him suggests that the exorcist is a disciple. The exorcist believes in Jesus enough to use his name successfully. Unlike the disciples, who could not exorcize the demon in the little boy, this exorcist has been able to cast out unclean spirits (9:38). Rather than hinder kingdom work by trying to erect boundaries that exclude, Jesus admonishes his followers to be at peace with one another (9:50).

The next episode addresses another low-status group in Mark's social world: women. When the Pharisees come to test Jesus, their question references the law, which only allows men the right to divorce (10:2–12). This practice leaves women vulnerable because they are financially and socially dependent on their husbands. Jesus declares that Moses allowed divorce because of their hard hearts. Quoting Gen. 1:27 and 2:24, he argues that divorce was not the original plan but a concession made due to their inability to live up to the original intent of Scripture. Jesus' words show that the Pharisees are not in line with teachings of Moses. When Jesus explains divorce to his disciples, he puts men and women on equal footing. His teaching gives both genders the same right to divorce as well as the same culpability should the divorced person remarry (9:10–12). Thus Mark continues to demonstrate the same concern for women he has shown with the positive portrayals of Peter's mother-in-law (1:31), the woman with the hemorrhage (5:25–34), and the Syrophoenician woman (7:26–30), as well as the intentional inclusion of "sister[s]" as part of Jesus' redefined family (3:35).

The narrative moves from the treatment of women to that of children. Jesus reiterates the principle of his last discipleship lesson. Greatness in the kingdom of God will not be the result of wealth, power, or ritual purity. On the contrary, the kingdom belongs to the least (10:14). This is precisely why one must become the least and servant of all to enter it (10:15). Jesus blesses the children (10:16), thereby sealing his reversal of the honor-shame codes. The ones who are blessed are the ones society has relegated to the lowest social level.

The last episode deals with wealth. The underlying issue is the treatment of another group considered least in Mark's social world, the poor. When a rich man approaches Jesus wanting to know how to gain eternal life (10:17), Jesus tells him to sell all he has, give the money to the poor, and then follow him (10:21). His command to give the money from the sold possessions is an attempt to restore to the poor what was unfairly taken from them. These instructions seek to remediate economic practices that consign the majority of the people to poverty. Discipleship that forbids the oppression of the poor protects these who are also among the least. Jesus' teaching about wealth runs counter to the prevailing notions of wealth in Mark's day. Wealth gave people access. Yet Jesus claims it is a hindrance to those who desire to enter the kingdom of God (10:23). Even for those who have little to no wealth, Jesus' declaration is so shocking that the disciples question the possibility of anyone being saved (10:26).

Despite Jesus' teaching on wealth and a third passion prediction, James and John still clamor for status by asking for positions of honor (10:37). Jesus presents his final discipleship lesson and again emphasizes the need to be a servant (10:43). He concludes by pointing out how he has modeled the behavior he is teaching them. He has not come to be served. Instead, he gives his life in service as he ministers to the least. He will give his life in death because the opposition to this ministry will be fatal. However, his service will ransom "many" (10:45), thereby releasing them from the "strong man's" clutches.

Mark finishes this section with the healing of blind Bartimaeus (10:46–52). He is the first person to call Jesus the "Son of David" (10:47–48) and thus to convey the political implications of Jesus' journey to Jerusalem. According to the Hebrew Scriptures, God promised the throne of Israel to David and his descendants forever (2 Sam. 7:16). It was therefore expected that the Messiah would be a descendant (son) of David (Isa. 11:1; Jer. 23:5–6). As son of David, Jesus is a threat to both Roman and Jewish leadership. The blind man sees the very thing that Jesus has foretold in his passion predictions.

The Text in the Interpretive Tradition

Jesus' passion predictions introduce a new theme into the Gospel: suffering. Since discipleship characterizes this portion of the Gospel, the relationship between suffering and discipleship is worth exploring. Historically, Mark scholars have understood suffering to be a condition or requirement of discipleship. Many interpret *dei* (8:31) as divine necessity. In other words, God sent Jesus to suffer. Others use this section of the Gospel as their interpretive key. They highlight themes of suffering and servanthood, and suffering and death. They claim that the key to understanding Jesus is in relation to his suffering and therefore describe him as a suffering Messiah. Others posit a scriptural necessity for suffering, by interpreting Mark 9:12 and 10:45 as allusions to Psalm 118 and Isaiah 53 respectively. Most recently, Mark scholars have argued for *dei* to be interpreted in terms of inevitability. They cite the opposition to Jesus' ministry in the narrative as the reason for his death. For these scholars, suffering is not a condition but a consequence of discipleship (St. Clair).

The Text in Contemporary Discussion

The relationship between suffering and discipleship is especially important for people who have endured personal or communal suffering. Womanist scholars have found it helpful to distinguish between suffering, on one hand, that arises from oppressive systems and circumstances and results in a static condition that will not change until its sources are confronted, and pain, on the other hand, that is a result of challenging the causes of one's oppression and therefore has the possibility of being eliminated. Jesus' passion is then understood in terms of pain. To follow him is not a call to perpetual suffering for the sake of suffering. To follow him is to accept pain as a consequence of discipleship that requires one to participate in boundary-breaking ministry like his (St. Clair, 145).

The work of womanist scholars causes exegetes (1) to be mindful, when interpreting passages about self-denial, of people who have been denied access to basic necessities, and (2) to be aware, when interpreting passages about taking up the cross, of people who have and are functioning as surrogates (persons who take the place of another by performing the roles and responsibilities of said person). How one interprets these passages may justify, prolong, or even sacralize the suffering and oppression that Jesus in Mark's Gospel seeks to eradicate.

Mark 11:1–12:44

Following to Jerusalem

The Text in Its Ancient Context

Jesus now arrives at Jerusalem, the center of Jewish religious power (11:1). His entry into the city is replete with messianic overtones. Jesus rides into Jerusalem on a colt. The scene depicts the fulfillment of Zech. 9:9. People spread their cloaks for Jesus to tread on like officers did when Jehu was anointed King (2 Kings 9:13). Hosanna, "save, please," conveys the people's desire for deliverance. It is clear from their shouts that they view Jesus' entry into the city as heralding the reinstitution of the Davidic monarchy (10:10). Like Bartimaeus, they recognize Jesus as the promised son of David. They quote Ps. 118:26 as they cry out, "Blessed is the one who comes in the name of Lord!" Yet the second portion of that verse, "we bless you from the house of the LORD," will not be realized. The ministry that has the crowds following him and his entry into the city amid cries of messianic expectation makes Jesus a threat to both Jewish and Roman leaders.

Mark adds new groups to those he has already shown to be arrayed against Jesus. The chief priests and the elders, whose rejection Jesus foretold in 8:31, confront him in the temple (11:27). The Sadducees join the chief priests, elders, scribes, Pharisees, and Herodians as interrogators of Jesus (12:18). The common link among them all is their support of and participation in the temple system, a system Jesus finds corrupt.

The temple is not functioning as intended. Therefore, one of Jesus' first undertakings is symbolically to cleanse the temple. He uses the language of the prophets to describe what has happened to the temple. Instead of being a "house of prayer for all nations" (Isa. 56:7), it has become "a den of robbers" (Jer. 7:11). In Mark, Jesus specifically uses the Greek word for "bandits" (*lēstai*). He equates temple practices with those of first-century highway robbers who plunder people by force. He also depicts Jesus as the stronger one who enters the strong man's house (3:27). And he uses the language of exorcism (*ekballein*) to describe the driving out of the buyers and sellers (11:15).

Additionally, Mark shows the temple system to be representative of a tree that does not produce fruit. He does this by "sandwiching" the temple cleansing (11:15–19) between the story of the cursed fig tree (11:12–14, 20–25). The temple is like the fig tree. It was the crowning achievement of Herod's building projects, but it only has the appearance of fruitfulness, like the fig tree in leaf suggests. On closer inspection, however, there is nothing to it. The fig tree imagery alludes to Old Testament Scriptures that compare Israel to barren fig trees (Jer. 13:13; Hosea 9:10; Mic. 7:1). Jesus' cursing of the fig tree, therefore, intimates the destruction of the temple.

The corrupt temple system and its impending demise is the result of corrupt leadership. In the parable of the vineyard (12:1–12), Jesus implicitly compares the scribes, chief priests, and elders to the evil tenants who kill the vineyard owner's beloved son (12:7–8). He warns people about the scribes' pride (12:38–9), unscrupulous financial practices that result in the "devouring" of widow's property (12:40), and hypocrisy (12:40). It is important to note that Mark uses the scribes to connect Jesus' enemies. He lists the scribes with the chief priests and elders (8:31; 11:27; 14:43, 53; 15:1) and with the Pharisees (7:1), whom Mark pairs with the Herodians (3:6; 12:13). Therefore, Jesus' condemnation of the scribes can be applied to all of the Jewish leaders whose opposition has increased in numbers and in intensity as the scribes and chief priests also look for a way to kill Jesus (11:18).

The Text in the Interpretive Tradition

Couched between Jesus' scathing condemnation of the scribes and his foretelling of the temple's destruction is the story of the widow's offering. Leo the Great, Gregory the Great, and John Chrysostom lifted her as an example of faith and generosity. Based on his interpretation of this story, Calvin concluded that one who "offers to God the little that he has, is more worthy of esteem than that of him who offers a hundred times more out of his abundance" (Calvin, 3:113). From their earliest readings until the present time, scholars have commended the widow whose actions Jesus is believed to have extolled. Most recently, however, scholars have interpreted this story as an indictment of the temple system that victimizes the poor and vulnerable.

The Text in Contemporary Discussion

In 2012, the *Chronicle of Philanthropy* reported their findings on giving patterns in the United States by state, city, and zip code. What they found was that people in higher-income brackets gave less to charitable causes than people with less income. Persons earning between $50,000 and 75,000 per year gave 7.6 percent of their income to charity. People earning more than $200,000 per year, and living in areas where at least 40 percent of their neighbors shared their economic status, gave only 2.8 percent to charity. The divide between income and generosity encourages us to take another look at the widow's offering in Mark's Gospel.

Much of contemporary discussion around this text no longer offers a commendation for the widow's gift but rather a condemnation of the systems of oppression, both religious and political, that persuade those with less to give out of their lack and the rich to keep what they have. They note the juxtaposition of Jesus' condemnation of the scribes as those who "devour widows' houses" (12:40) and the story of the widow's offering. The widow is now seen as a victim of predatory practices rather than a woman whose faith in God results in generosity. Her once positive portrayal is threatened as she becomes a passive character who is duped into supporting something that Jesus condemns and predicts will be destroyed.

As we interpret and apply this passage to our current context, it is important to tease out the strands of condemnation and commendation. How we understand the relationship between the woman and the temple influences how we use this passage to either encourage or discourage relationship between giver and the faith community to which they give.

Mark 13:1–37

Following to the End

The Text in Its Ancient Context

Chapter 13 contains the largest block of teaching found in Mark's Gospel. Commentators have referred to this chapter as the prophetic discourse, believing it to foretell the future; the eschatological discourse, because it speaks of "the end"; the Olivet Discourse, because Mount Olives is the setting for the passage (Brooks, 204); and the "Little Apocalypse," because it reveals the future and discloses the heavenly realm. The description of this chapter as the Little Apocalypse, however, is often debated because certain apocalyptic features such as visions, resurrection, and final judgment are missing. Neither is there a juxtaposition between heaven and earth, the present age and the age to come, or those inside and outside of the church that characterize Christian apocalyptic writings (Edwards, 384). In addition, there is no heavenly intermediary revealing the future events.

Although Mark 13 is different from most examples of apocalyptic literature, there are enough features to categorize it as such. Since apocalyptic literature is a form of sociopolitical resistance by people who have little chance of achieving the political, economic, or military overthrow of their oppressors, Mark, written in the context of the Jewish War, reflects the exact setting out of which apocalyptic literature develops. Moreover, the description of wars, conflicts among nations and kingdoms, famines, and earthquakes are common Christian and Jewish apocalyptic features. Mark specifies that Jesus teaches from the Mount of Olives, the eschatological location of YHWH's final deliverance of Israel from her enemies (Zech. 14:4). Mark 13:19 parallels Dan. 12:1, which is an undisputed apocalyptic portion of the book. Both Mark and Daniel foretell suffering using the same Greek word, *thlipsis*, and record the magnitude of the suffering in similar fashion. Daniel states that it is "such as never occurred since the nations existed"; Mark says it is "such as has not been from the beginning of the creation."

Because apocalyptic literature arises from situations of oppression and/or persecution, its writers often promote both patient endurance and hope. In a manner of speaking, apocalyptic literature is "good news," not in the sense of a literary genre but in terms of the message it proclaims. There is confidence in the fact that although things look bleak now, God is in control and will be victorious. Therefore, Jesus encourages the disciples to "endure" (13:13) and "keep awake" (13:35, 37). The events Jesus foretells in verses 5–23 are described as "birth pangs" (13:8). Read in this context, Mark communicates to his readers that while their situation will get worse before it gets better, their suffering is connected to a greater purpose (Juel, 176). It is not the end; their salvation is (13:13). Mark thus inspires a present hope in his readers as he communicates Jesus' revelation of future events.

It is important to note that some apocalyptic literature "describes the course of history as well as a climactic cosmic transformation" (Donahue and Harrington, 378). In other words, one of the functions of apocalyptic literature is to explain the current circumstances of its readers in light of God's unfolding plan. As expectations for liberation erupted into social protests such as banditry and messianic movements (Horsley 1984, 482), messianic expectations raised eschatological hope, since the Messiah was expected to arrive before "the end." Therefore, Mark needed to address these first-century Palestinian expectations while protecting his community (13:5–6, 21–22). The warnings against false prophets and messianic pretenders found on Jesus' lips frame the discourse so that Mark's readers will not be led astray (13:6, 22).

According to Mark, Jesus foretells the destruction of the temple (13:2) as well as the persecution of his followers (13:9, 11–12). These prophecies prepare Mark's readers for their current state of affairs. First, they are reassured that the temple was not intended to be the center of the community's faith. Mark presses this point by reminding them (through words he attributes to Jesus) that those in Judea are supposed to flee when the temple's destruction, signaled by the "desolating sacrilege," is about to take place (13:14). In Dan. 9:27, the "desolating sacrilege" referred to the pagan altar set up in the temple by Antiochus Epiphanes. Mark uses the phrase to refer to another desecration of the sacred space. By using the masculine form of the Greek participle for "stand" (*estēkota*) rather than the neuter, Mark informs his readers that the "desolating sacrilege" is not an "it" but a "he." There are three main proposals for identifying this person: (1) Caligula, who ordered the erection of a statue of himself in the temple in 40 CE (Josephus, *Ant.* 18.261), (2) the rebel Eleazar, who used the inner temple as his headquarters from the winter of 67–68 CE until 70 CE, and (3) Titus, who entered the temple in 70 CE as it was being destroyed. Since the "desolating sacrilege" is a sign to flee Judea, Caligula would be too early and Titus would be too late, which leaves Eleazar as the best option (Marcus). The attention Mark pays to the "course of history," namely, the temple's destruction and the desolating sacrilege, provides clues for dating his Gospel as well.

By recounting Jesus' prophecy about the persecution of his followers, Mark parallels his community's suffering with that of Jesus. Like Jesus, they will be "handed over to councils" (15:1), beaten (14:65), brought to trial (14:55–64) and before governors (15:1–15), and betrayed by their own families (14:43–45). Given Jesus' redefinition of family (3:35), the betrayal by family members may not come from one's biological kin but those who are part of the community of disciples.

After twenty-three verses that focus on the "course of history," Jesus' discourse gives way to "cosmic transformation." In the background of Jesus' teaching is the disciples' question of when "these things" will take place (13:4). The contextual referent for "these things" is the destruction of the temple. However, as Jesus answers their question, he speaks of "the end" twice (13:7,13) and concludes with the appearance of the son of man and the gathering of the elect (13:24–27). The son of man's appearance in Mark 13:26 mirrors that of the apocalyptic son of man who also comes in the clouds in Dan. 7:13.

Although his style is not typical of apocalyptic literature, Mark does juxtapose heaven and earth in his own way. The destruction of the temple signals transformation on an earthly scale, but the appearance of the son of man does so on a celestial scale. Famines, earthquakes, and wars are signs on earth that will eventually give way to the heavenly signs of a darkened sun, a lightless moon, falling stars, and shaken heavenly powers. Thus salvation takes on a spiritual, eschatological dimension as those who "endure to the end will be saved" (13:13).

Ultimately, the disciples' question is never answered. Jesus informs them that he does not know when "that day or hour" (13:32) will come. Instead, he tells them how to interpret the events so that they know when he is "near, at the very gate" (13:29). However, Jesus does tell them that it will not happen before the good news is preached to all nations (13:10). This statement extends the timetable of Jesus' return for Mark's readers. It reminds them that the end is imminent but not yet. Therefore, he tells them what to do: "Watch" (13:5, 9, 23, 33, *blepete*).

"Watch" characterizes Mark's ethical stance (Donahue and Harrington, 378). The inclusion of this ethical/exhortation component makes this chapter practical and immediately applicable. It also caused James A. Brooks to conclude that Mark 13 "combines two literary forms, apocalyptic and testamental" (Brooks, 204). This fusion enables Mark to achieve his purpose for this chapter: keep eschatological hope alive while balancing it with vigilance (Donahue and Harrington, 378). His message to his readers is clear: This is not the end. It is only birth pangs, and they are just as unpredictable as labor. So, keep awake!

The Text in the Interpretive Tradition

In Mark 13:32, Jesus states that he does not know the day or hour of the son of man's return. This statement resulted in three words, "nor the Son," becoming a point of interpretive contention since its earliest readings. For interpreters such as Arius, this verse posed no problems. Instead, they saw it as scriptural affirmation of their theological position that subordinated both the Son and the Holy Spirit to the Father.

Using Mark 13:32 (and its parallel Matt. 24:36), they rejected the equal divinity of Jesus with the Father. However, the majority of interpretations of this verse have been fueled by the same discomfort as described by John Calvin: "But since it is manifest that the same kind of ignorance is ascribed to Christ as is ascribed *to the angels*, we must endeavor to find some other meaning which is more suitable" (Calvin, 1845, 3:37).

The quest for a "more suitable" meaning began with Matthew's Gospel. Although the most reliable manuscripts of Matthew's parallel text (Matt. 24:36) include "nor the Son," several omit the phrase due to the doctrinal problems it raised (Harrington, 342). Athanasius, who defended the doctrine of the Trinity against the Arian heresy of subordinationism, affirmed the divinity of Jesus by arguing that Jesus was "speaking according to his humanity" in this verse. Chrysostom, Gregory of Nazianzus, Martin Luther, and John Wesley also espoused this interpretation of Mark 13:32. Ambrose seems to have had the Matthew text with the omission of "nor the Son" since he accused the Arians of inserting the phrase into Mark's text because the other Gospels did not include it.

For Augustine, the issue was not from which nature Jesus' words derived, but an exercise of choice. Jesus chose not to disclose what he knew because "he had not been sent by the Father with this commission, so long as he lived among mortals." Theophylact concurred, reasoning that this concealment was "better for us; for if, now that we know not the end, we are careless, what should we do if we knew it?" Hilary of Poitiers argued that Jesus' apparent lack of knowledge was not a reflection of his ignorance, but that it "must be connected with the hiding of the treasures of wisdom, which are in Him." Contemporary options for those who take Mark literally follow one of the three interpretive trajectories: subordinationism, in which Jesus (and by implication the Holy Spirit) are ignorant of the Father's timetable; "official ignorance," in which Jesus purposely conceals the day and hour; or what might be called the "nonuse" approach, in which Jesus does not use the omniscience of his divine nature but rather speaks from a human point of view (Carl).

The Text in Contemporary Discussion

The material in the first twenty-three verses of Mark 13 can be linked easily to events shortly before or after the fall of the Jerusalem temple. However, verses 24–27 foretell the coming of the son of man, an event that has not yet occurred. On one end of a spectrum today are readers who have interpreted Mark 13 in its ancient setting and concluded that Jesus expected the fulfillment of verses 24–27 in his lifetime, but died a failure (Schweitzer). On the other end are premillennialists, who read Rev. 20:1–6 literally and believe that Jesus will physically return to rapture the righteous prior to the tribulation and that he will subsequently inaugurate a thousand-year reign. They see the signs of Jesus' coming in contemporary events.

During the twentieth century, the possibility of nuclear destruction, the reality of ecological collapse, the creation of the state of Israel along with the Six Day and Yom Kippur Wars, and the perceived threats to US exceptionalism fueled premillennial expectations of Jesus' return. Despite the statement in 13:32 that the timing of the son of man's return remains a mystery, some readers still attempt to correlate current events with those listed in Mark 13 so as to describe contemporary timetables that will lead up to Jesus' appearing. Examples in popular culture include *The Late, Great Planet Earth* (Lindsey 1970) and, more recently, the *Left Behind* series (LaHaye and Jenkins 1995-2007).

The underlying premise of such interpretations is the expectation that apocalyptic passages like Mark 13 accurately and precisely predict the future. Should supposedly predicted events not take place as expected, then the passage might become a failed apocalyptic text or proof that Jesus was wrong (Schweitzer). Yet, premillennialists like Tim LaHaye and Hal Lindsey can avoid Schweitzer's conclusion if the events that signal "the end" are seen as still forthcoming. If Jesus does not return as expected, then calendars can be readjusted. This way, the *interpretation of the text*, rather than the text itself, fails. The "prophet," rather than Jesus, is wrong. However, this attempt fails to preserve the integrity of the text. Instead, it risks undermining the text's integrity by using current events to predict the "end," when the historical context of Mark's Gospel points to the events surrounding the Jewish War.

Mark 14:1–15:47

The Cost of Following

The Text in Its Ancient Context

Mark gives great attention to Jesus' passion. He lays the foundation for his passion narrative with three passion predictions and then devotes one third of his Gospel to detailing Jesus' final days. He takes great pains to highlight what contemporary readers might identify as the sociopolitical reasons behind Jesus' death. Although Jesus is executed by Rome as a criminal, his death does not represent a failure on his part. Rather, Mark shows that there has been a failure of justice, a failure of discipleship, and a failure of sight on the part of Roman and Jewish leadership.

Mark tells the story of Jesus' death against the backdrop of the Passover. The day before the feast, the day of preparation, the chief priests and scribes are preparing to arrest Jesus (14:1). A woman enters the room where Jesus is sharing a meal with Simon the leper and anoints him (14:3). Amid criticisms for wasting the money on the perfume and accusations of neglecting the poor, Jesus defends her actions. Jesus states that the deed was done "for me" (14:6). Just as the disciples' lack of fasting while the "bridegroom" is present (2:18–20) showed an understanding of the significance of Jesus' presence among them, so this woman's kindness highlights the same (Myers, 359). Moreover, acts of kindness can be shown to the poor at any time, but he will not always be with them (14:7). His statement is neither a consignment of people to perpetual poverty nor an encouragement to neglect the poor. Jesus does not set up an "either/or" dynamic. Personal acts of kindness are no substitute for public care of the poor or vice versa, and "one should not be harassed for doing either" (Tolbert, 271). By performing a "good service," this nameless, speechless woman fits the predominant image of women in Mark's Gospel as those who serve and provide for Jesus

(1:31; 15:41). Her prophetic act helps to move the reader into Mark's passion narrative. She is not anointing Jesus as king but is preparing his body "beforehand for its burial" (14:8). Jesus will not be given a crown, but a cross.

The Last Supper (14:17–25); Jesus' betrayal (14:41–45), arrest (14:46–49), and trial before the Sanhedrin (14:53–65); his prayer in Gethsemane (14:32–40); the desertion of his disciples (14:50–52); and Peter's denial (14:66–72) all occur on the day of Passover. The Passover is not simply a remembrance of divine intervention, but of divine intervention with sociopolitical implications. It is a Jewish feast that commemorates Israel's liberation from Egyptian slavery or the freeing of God's people from an oppressive government. Just as the Passover celebrates the ransoming of Israel from Egypt (Exod. 6:6, *lytroō*), so Mark presents Jesus' life and death as part of a ransoming work (10:45, *lytron*). This time, the oppressive regime is Rome.

During the Passover meal, Jesus reinterprets the bread and wine in light of his impending death. The bread is his body, which will soon be broken (14:22). The wine is the "blood of the covenant" (14:24). The "blood of the covenant" has two possible references to the exodus story. First, it may refer to the blood that Israelites painted on their doorposts to protect their firstborn from the death angel (Exod. 12:7). According to Exod. 4:22, Israel is God's firstborn. Therefore, Jesus intimates that the deliverance and protection of Israel is tied to his spilled blood. The second reference to the "blood of the covenant" is the blood sprinkled on the Israelites at Sinai to establish their relationship as the people of God and confirm their covenant with God (24:1–8). Jesus' spilled blood verifies that God's commitment to Israel is still in effect. However, Mark shows that what God is doing through the death of Jesus will not be for Israel alone. Instead, he once again pushes for gentile inclusion.

Israel's deliverance from Egyptian slavery was necessary for God to fulfill God's promise of land and progeny to Abraham (Gen. 15:5–7). According to Gen. 17:5, Abraham would not be the ancestor of the Israelites alone, but of "many [*pollōn*] nations" (Gen. 17:5). Mark links the language of the "many" (*polloi*) to Jesus. Jesus will give his life as a ransom for "many" (10:45, *polloi*). His blood is described as being "poured out for many" (14:24, *polloi*).

It is important to note that the Passover language in Mark is not expiatory; it points instead to the sociopolitical dimensions of Jesus' death (Blount). Mark simply states that Jesus' body is broken. Unlike Luke, he does not add "for you" (Luke 22:19). Moreover, the breaking and blessing of the bread alludes to the feeding stories in which Jews (6:33–44) and gentiles (8:1–9) are filled. In addition, the "blood of the covenant" is not specified as being for the "forgiveness of sins" (as in Matt. 26:28). Jesus forgave sin prior to his death (Mark 2:5).

At the heart of the animosity toward Jesus on the part of scribes, Pharisees, and other authorities in Jerusalem are the sociopolitical implications of his ministry. Jesus is a threat to the temple system and their control of the people, both of which ingratiate them to Rome. When Jesus is arrested, the only accusation Mark records is someone claiming that Jesus said, "I will destroy this temple that is made with hands, and in three days I will build another, not made with hands" (14:58). When Jesus drove the animal sellers and money-changers out of the temple, it resulted in the chief priests and scribes looking for a way to kill him (11:18). Jesus has predicted the temple's destruction (13:1–2). Later, when he dies, Mark will report that the temple curtain is torn (*eschisthē*) in two (15:38) like the heavens were ripped asunder (*schizomenous*) during Jesus' baptism (1:10). Because the tearing of the temple curtain occurs during the darkness that covers the land at noonday (15:33), it is probably best read as an omen of God's judgment against the temple. However, Mark's use of *schizein* at both Jesus' baptism and death suggests that the latter event, like the former, grants access to God, rather than the temple system. Moreover, the tearing (*schizein*) of the curtain suggests that the breach between the old way represented by the temple and the new way represented by Jesus is as irreparable as the tear (*schizma*) created from sewing together new and old cloth (2:21).

Such bold political counteractions require authority. At Jesus' trial before the Sanhedrin, the high priest's question is therefore one about identity. He asks if Jesus is "the Messiah [*christos*], the Son of the Blessed One?" (14:61). The high priest's question mimics what Mark has already told his readers is Jesus' true identity. According to Mark, Jesus is the Messiah (*christos*, a political designation), and the Son of God (a theological designation, 1:1). Jesus affirms both by responding with an answer that has political and theological undertones. He begins with "I am" (*egō eimi*), which is a play on the divine name (Exod. 3:14) revealed to Moses during his divine commission to free Israel from Egyptian bondage. Next, Jesus declares that those questioning him will see him "seated at the right hand of the Power" (14:62). For Jesus' interrogators, his position next to God may be seen as a threat to the sovereignty and/or the oneness of God. In either case, they view him as "infringing on God's prerogatives" (Juel, 208–9). Consequently, they charge him with blasphemy, which is punishable by death. Yet they take Jesus to the Roman procurator, Pilate (15:1), where the accusation against Jesus becomes purely political, not theological. In an effort to present Jesus' offense as a crime punishable by Rome, blasphemy disappears from everyone's vocabulary. Instead, the charge is treason: his alleged claim to be a king. Three times Pilate refers to him as "king of the Jews" (15:2, 9, 12). The crowds as well as "the whole cohort" mock him as such (15:16–20). The sign placed over his cross reads the same (15:26). Even the chief priests and scribes refer to him using two political titles: "king of Israel," a variant of "king of the Jews," and "Messiah" (15:32).

Mark further highlights the sociopolitical nature of Jesus' death through his use of bandit (*lēstēs*) language. In first-century Palestine, bandits were typically highway robbers or guerrilla warriors who opposed Rome and Judean collaborators with Rome. They were viewed by Rome and Roman sympathizers as seditious and traitors (Horsley 1985). When taken into custody, Jesus likens his arrest to that of a bandit (14:48). Mark tells us that he was crucified between two bandits (15:27). Moreover, Mark juxtaposes Jesus and Barabbas. Jesus is arrested as if he were the rebel; Barabbas has been arrested for actually participating in an insurrection. There is no historical evidence that attests to the existence of Barabbas or the Passover custom that allows the crowd to choose which man goes free. Jesus and Barabbas may be Mark's way of representing two sociopolitical responses to Roman oppression. Jesus represents those in favor of nonviolent opposition. Barabbas, whom Myers says is described by Mark as a Sicarii operative, is the choice of those who advocate outright rebellion to Rome (Myers, 380). Meanwhile, Jewish leaders who have made the temple a den of bandits (11:17) are behind Jesus' arrest.

In the end, Jesus is crucified. He suffers a horrifically painful and humiliating death reserved for crimes against the state, high treason, and as punishment for slaves, prisoners of war, rebels, robbers, freedmen, and *peregrini*, that is, free persons without Roman citizenship (Hengel). Mark shows Jesus' death to be a failure of justice. The Sanhedrin does not follow jurisprudence found in the Torah (or, later, the Mishnah), nor does Pilate free him when he believes Jesus to be innocent (Juel). Jesus' death highlights the failure of his followers, who cannot stay awake and pray with him in Gethsemane (14:37); who betray him (14:10, 43), desert him (14:50), deny him (14:66–72), turn against him (15:14), and follow only from a great distance (15:40–41). Mark uses verbal irony to reveal the failure of sight on the part of Jewish and Roman leadership. They repeatedly identify him correctly as "King of the Jews," but fail to recognize who he really is.

However, none of these failures come as a surprise to Jesus, nor should they surprise Mark's readers. Jesus has predicted it all, and so it has come to pass. Yet one things remains to be accomplished: a resurrection!

The Text in the Interpretive Tradition

Readings of Mark's passion narrative have often been influenced by the ransom and the substitutionary/penal-substitutionary theories of atonement. Scholars who argue for a theory of atonement in Mark's Gospel point to 10:45 and 14:24 as justification for their position. In addition, some read Mark's passion narrative against the backdrop of

Isaiah 53 and contend that Mark presents Jesus as Isaiah's Suffering Servant. Jesus then becomes one who suffers vicariously for humanity as payment for our sin. Once one assumes an atonement theory is at play, one interprets other portions of the Gospel in light of the theory rather than the narrative context. For example, Morna Hooker interprets Jesus' "cry of dereliction" (15:34) as his experiencing "what Paul elsewhere describes as 'becoming a curse' (Gal. 3:13) or 'being made sin' (2 Cor. 5:21)" (Hooker, 375).

In the last thirty years, however, scholars have argued against the presence of any atonement theories in Mark. Instead, they opt to make meaning of Jesus' death on the basis of evidence within the text rather than by imposing theological constructs formulated outside it (Myers; Tolbert; Blount). Therefore, Mark 15:34 can be explained within the context of the narrative using the historical reality of the crucifixion as its backdrop. The cry of dereliction becomes "Jesus' final emotional and psychological torment, in addition to his physical suffering" (Powery, 150). By quoting Psalm 22:1 and alluding to Psalm 22 throughout the passion narrative, Mark holds in tension the horrific conditions of Jesus' death and the hope for his vindication as a righteous sufferer.

The Text in Contemporary Discussion

The shift to a narrative reading of Mark as described above also enables us to recognize Christian anti-Judaism in Mark's Gospel. Mark portrays the Jewish leadership (3:6; 11:18; 14:1; 15:11) and the crowds (14:43; 15:8–14) as the instigators of Jesus' death, causing some to conclude that Mark's Gospel is inherently antisemitic. William A. Johnson argues that "every kind of Jew" is presented negatively in the Gospel, which he describes as a "carefully devised theological attack on the Jews" (Johnson, 183). He concurs with S. G. F. Brandon that Mark's reader "is led to see Jesus as both rejected by, and in turn rejecting his fellow-Jews" (Brandon, 274). Fortunately, this shift to narrative readings has also sensitized scholars to the potential antisemitic implications of their analyses. Therefore, attention is given to certain aspects of the Gospel in an effort to prevent readers from forming antisemitic attitudes based on Mark's story.

Contemporary scholars note that Mark's Gospel reflects the historical tensions between Jews who followed Jesus and Jews who did not in Mark's day (Hooker, 24). Initially, the dispute between Jews and Jewish Christians was an internal dispute among *Jews* about accepting Jesus as the Messiah. Thus Mark writes about a time when followers of Jesus will be "beaten in synagogues" (13:9).

In addition, scholars highlight Jesus' Jewish background. Indeed, Jesus was a Jew whose ministry was directed to the Jewish people. His use of Scripture and adherence to the law (1:44; 3:4; 10:19; 12:29–31) demonstrate his fidelity to Judaism. The main contention with his opponents over Mosaic tradition was whether he or they were more faithful in interpretation and application (Hooker, 24–25).

Narrative readings of Mark's Gospel are also careful to point out the divergence between historical data and Mark's story. Historically, Jesus' death cannot be attributed to the Jewish leaders as Mark portrays. Scholars appeal to extrabiblical literature to see if the image of the easily manipulated Pilate in Mark's Gospel matches what other writers say about him. It seems highly unlikely that Pilate would have left the decision to execute Jesus to the crowd, especially since there is no extrabiblical evidence of any custom to release a prisoner of the crowd's choosing (15:8). Legally, Pilate would have had to sentence Jesus to death, and the means of Jesus' death—crucifixion—was a Roman practice, not a Jewish one.

Contra Johnson, Mark does not present all of the Jews in a negative light. Mark's Gospel distinguishes itself with a very positive portrayal of women, the majority of which are Jewish, who serve as examples of discipleship (Dewey; Malbon 1983; Miller; Kinukawa; Mitchell). Jairus, a synagogue leader, had enough faith to have his petition granted (5:36) and be allowed to remain in the room after Jesus put everyone out (5:40). Although Jesus' disciples betray, deny, and desert him, he still commands them to meet him in Galilee after the resurrection (16:7).

Mark 16:1–8

Will You Follow?

The Text in Its Ancient Context

Despite the variety of endings given to Mark, the evidence suggests that the version of Mark's Gospel available to his original readers ended with 16:8 (see below). Chapter 16 begins with three women journeying to Jesus' tomb at first light (16:1–2). Mary Magdalene heads the list of women. Mark tells us that she provided for Jesus' ministry and witnessed his crucifixion (15:40), followed to see where he was buried (15:47), and came to anoint his body (16:1). Absent is any reference to her deliverance from seven demons (Luke 8:2) or any information that would suggest she was the harlot that the later interpretive and especially artistic tradition claimed. There is some inconsistency around the identity of "Mary, the mother of James." It is not certain whether she is also "Mary, mother of James and Joses" (15:40), "Mary, mother of Joses" (15:47), or even Mary, Jesus' mother, who is mentioned with Jesus' brothers, also named James and Joses (6:3). Salome only appears here and in 15:40, among those who provided for Jesus' ministry and were present at the crucifixion. These women anticipate providing for Jesus one last time. They come to anoint his body, apparently oblivious to the fact that he was "anointed beforehand for [his] burial" in Bethany (14:3–9). Yet, even the narration of Jesus' predicting his own death and resurrection three times (8:31; 9:31; 10:33–34), the first being declared "quite openly" (8:32), had not caused them to expect a resurrection, only a dead body.

The timing of the women's visit is also inconsistent. "Early morning" would have been between three and six in the morning. Nevertheless, Mark adds that they came after sunrise, perhaps wishing to assure his readers that the women were able to see clearly what follows. As they journey to the tomb, they worry about the stone at its entrance (16:3). The stone, however, is an afterthought, as they do all the preparations for the anointing and depart for the tomb, thinking about the stone only as they arrive. This afterthought, Hooker asserts, is probably an attempt to emphasize the fact that the tomb was indeed sealed (Hooker, 384) and to confirm that the absence of Jesus' body is due to a resurrection, not a theft.

When the women arrive at the tomb, the stone has already been rolled away (16:4). However, there is no resurrection appearance, only a young man with a message. Mark describes him as a "young man dressed in a white robe" (16:5). Some interpreters identify the young man as an angel, citing his white robe; the similarity between the women's alarm at seeing the young man and the fear that often accompanies angelic appearances (Gen. 21:17; Matt. 28:5; Luke 1:13, 30; 2:10); Luke's (24:4) and Josephus's (*Ant.* 5.277) use of the word "man" (*anēr*) to describe angelic appearances; and the fact that the young man knows about the postresurrection meeting in Galilee (14:28)—information R. T. France argues no human being apart from the disciples would have known (France, 676). Others, however, link the young man in the tomb to the young man in the garden who lost his garment during Jesus' arrest.

The Greek words used for "young man" (*neaniskos*) and "dressed" (*peribeblēmenos*) occur only here (16:5) and in 14:51–52. Mark connected Jesus with the young man in the garden, writing that the latter "followed" (*synēkolouthe*) Jesus. (Throughout the Gospel, Mark uses "follow" [*akolouthein*] to signify discipleship: 1:17, 20; 2:14, 15; 3:7; 5:24, 37; 6:1; 8:34; 10:21, 28, 32, 52; 11:9; 14:54; 15:41. By adding the preposition *syn* to the word, Mark suggests a close relationship between the young man and Jesus.) Both are dressed in linen fabric, the young man wearing a linen cloth (*sindon*) when Jesus is arrested (14:51) and Jesus wrapped in a linen cloth (*sindon*) before Joseph places him in the tomb (15:46). Mark also links Jesus with the young man in the tomb, recording that both appear in white garments: Jesus in "dazzling white" at the transfiguration (9:3) and the young man in the tomb (16:5).

Finally, Mark specifies the location of the young man in the tomb as being "seated on the right" (16:5). Individuals positioned on the right side figure prominently in Mark's Gospel: James and John request to sit at the right and left of Jesus (10:40); the Messiah's place is at the right hand of the Lord according to Ps. 110:1 quoted in Mark 12:36; and Jesus prophesies the coming of the son of man "seated at the right hand of the Power" (14:62). Myers defines the right side as denoting "true power of solidarity" (Myers, 397). Although there is no scholarly consensus on the identity of either young man (in the garden or at the tomb), the connections Mark makes between them and Jesus suggest that the young man was someone close enough to Jesus to have insider information and familiar enough to Mark's community to need no explanation.

The young man tells the women that "Jesus of Nazareth" has been raised (16:5–6). He does not employ a christological title, but rather situates Jesus historically as a real man from a real place. The women are commanded to carry the news to Jesus' disciples "and Peter" (16:7). It is most likely that the young man mentions Peter by name because Peter needs special encouragement (Juel, 232). As one who denied being a disciple by denying Jesus (Hooker, 385), he is specifically welcomed back here into the community of followers.

Unlike the people in the Gospel who are commanded to be quiet but tell what Jesus has done anyway (1:44; 7:36), the women who are commanded to speak here remain quiet. Mark highlights this with a double negative construction in Greek: "they said nothing to no one" (16:8). Instead, the women flee like the disciples (14:50–52). Narratively, there is a failure of discipleship for all who have followed Jesus. Yet the fact that Mark's community has access to his Gospel proves that someone said something. The message was indeed proclaimed.

Neither the absence of a resurrection appearance nor the fear and silence of the women nullifies Mark's description of his work as "good news." Emerson Powery states that for Mark, "hope is not defined by a resurrection or a physical appearance *but* by an empty tomb and a promised re-gathering" (Powery, 152). Herein lies the good news: not only is the tomb empty, but Jesus also has gone ahead of them to Galilee, "just as he said" (14:28; 16:7). There is no need to doubt Jesus' words, as Mark has taken great pains to prove his trustworthiness. His instructions concerning his entry into Jerusalem (11:2–6), the preparation for the

Passover meal (14:16), and the events surrounding the passion have all come to pass (Juel, 233). Moreover, Mark has kept his word. He promised to tell "the beginning of the good news of Jesus Christ." Whether by accident or intent, this is exactly what he has done.

The Text in the Interpretive Tradition

Interpretations of Mark's last chapter must contend with a problem unique to his Gospel. The Gospel has four endings: 16:8, the longer ending (vv. 9–20), a shorter ending, and the longer and shorter endings combined. The most reliable codices, Sinaiticus and Vaticanus, end with 16:8. Both Clement of Alexandria and Origen knew only of this ending. However, Eusebius and Jerome report that they are aware of the longer ending, but the longer ending is not found in the majority of Greek manuscripts. Both Irenaeus, who quotes 16:19, and Tatian, who includes the longer ending in his *Diatessaron*, do so without any acknowledgment of its being a later addition. By the second century, either the longer and/or shorter endings were added and were copied onto the majority of manuscripts.

In 1546, the Council of Trent canonized the old Latin Vulgate edition, which included Mark's longer ending. The Protestants also accepted the longer ending by including it in the King James Version. Modern scholarship reverted to the ending at 16:8 after Adolf von Harnack contended, in 1893, that Mark's original ending was lost. The textual evidence above as well as the stylistic, syntactical, vocabulary, and theological differences between the material prior to and after 16:8 have been the basis for contemporary arguments in favor of an ending at 16:8.

Whereas some of the earliest readers of the Gospel felt it necessary to create an ending for Mark's Gospel that is more consistent with the endings of Matthew, Luke, and John, contemporary readers may find the ending at 16:8 to be theologically consistent with the preceding narrative. Unlike von Harnack, they may consider that Mark intentionally ended his Gospel at 16:8. Donald Juel argues that the ending at 16:8

leaves the reader without any reason to trust human response: one "can only trust that God will one day finish the story, as God has promised" (Juel, 235). Others may see the abruptness of 16:8, with its unusual grammatical structure, to be an invitation by the author for readers to finish his story of discipleship for themselves. Early readers did something similar, codifying their supplemental endings by including them in ancient manuscripts. Contemporary readers will have to decide how they will complete "the beginning of the good news of Jesus Christ, the Son of God" (1:1).

The Text in Contemporary Discussion

Traditional African American preaching lends homiletical support to Mark's Gospel being good news despite the ending at 16:8. In *Celebration and Experience in Preaching*, Henry Mitchell argued that celebration, which has been defined as "the joyful and ecstatic reinforcement of the truth already taught and delivered in the main body of the sermon" (Thomas, 85), is a distinctive of African American preaching (Mitchell 1990). In the overwhelming majority of African American sermons, the moment of celebration centers on the resurrection of Jesus. However, the celebration often begins, like Mark's passion narrative, with a detailed account of the crucifixion. Classic African American preaching often punctuates the story with rhetorical questions like "He died, didn't he die?" and describe how Jesus was "hung high and stretched wide" until "the earth reeled and rocked like a drunken man, and the sun refused to shine." At this point, worshipers are often already standing on their feet, clapping their hands, shouting the preacher on, or engaged in some other form of congregational celebration in response to the Word. This celebration is not a reflection of masochistic or death-glorifying tendencies but a manifestation of the congregant's confidence in the end of the story.

Like Mark's community, the worshipers are not physical witnesses to Jesus' resurrection. However, the proclamation of it is enough to elicit praise because the one who foretold it and the witness of other believers are enough. There is every reason to expect death to give way to life, even in the midst of the darkest circumstances. So, before the preacher can say "early Sunday morning," the celebration has begun. It is not based on what people did but on what God did. They believe God raised Jesus from the dead, even if they have not yet seen the risen Lord. They do not need to end the story. Instead, they can be a part of it, by following the resurrected one.

WORKS CITED

Blevins, James L. 1974. "Seventy-Two Years of the Messianic Secret: A Review Article." *Perspectives in Religious Studies* 1, no. 2:192–200.

Blount, Brian K. 1998. *Go Preach! Mark's Kingdom Message and the Black Church Today*. Maryknoll, NY: Orbis.

Brandon, S. G. F. 1967. *Jesus and the Zealots*. New York: Oxford University Press.

Brooks, James A. 1991. *Mark*. The New American Commentary 23. Nashville: Broadman & Holman.

Burkett, Delbert. 1999. *The Son of Man Debate: A History and Evaluation*. New York: Cambridge University Press.

Calvin, John. 1845. *Commentary on a Harmony of the Evangelists Matthew, Mark, and Luke* (Vols. 2 and 3). Trans. the Rev. William Pringle. Edinburgh: The Calvin Translation Society.

Carl, Harold F. 2001. "Only the Father Knows: Historical and Evangelical Responses to Jesus' Eschatological Ignorance in Mark 13:32." *Journal of Biblical Studies* 1, no. 3. http://www.mountainretreatorg.net/articles/only_the_father_knows.shtml.

Collins, Adela Yarbro. 1992. *The Beginning of the Gospel: Probings of Mark in Context*. Minneapolis: Fortress Press.

Dewey, Joanna. 2006. "Women in the Gospel of Mark." *WW* 26, no. 1:22–29.

Donahue, John R., and Daniel J. Harrington. 2002. *The Gospel of Mark*. Sacra Pagina 2. Collegeville, MN: Liturgical Press.

Driscoll, Mark. 2006. *Confessions of a Reformission Rev.: Hard Lessons from an Emerging Missional Church*. Grand Rapids: Zondervan.

Dunn, James D. G. 1970. "The Messianic Secret in Mark." *TynBul* 21:92–117.

Edwards, James R. 2002. *The Gospel according to Mark*. Pillar New Testament Commentary. Grand Rapids: Eerdmans.

France, R. T. 2003. *Divine Government: God's Kingship in the Gospel of Mark*. Vancouver, BC: Regent College Publishing.

Haber, Susan. 2003. "A Woman's Touch: Feminist Encounters with the Hemorrhaging Woman in Mark 5:24-34." *JSNT* 26 no. 2:171–92.

Hanson, K. C. 1997. "The Galilean Fishing Economy and the Jesus Tradition." *BTB* 27:99–111.

Harrington, Daniel J. 1991. *The Gospel of Matthew*. Sacra Pagina. Collegeville, MN: Liturgical Press.

Hengel, Martin. 1977. *Crucifixion*. Minneapolis: Fortress Press.

Hooker, Morna D. 1999. *The Gospel according to St. Mark*. Peabody, MA: Hendrickson.

Horsley, Richard A. 1984. "Popular Messianic Movements around the Time of Jesus." *CBQ* 46:471–95.

Horsley, Richard A. 1985. *Bandits, Prophets, and Messiahs: Popular Movements at the Time of Jesus*. Harrisburg, PA: Trinity Press International.

Johnson, William A. 1989. " 'The Jews' in Saint Mark's Gospel." *Religion and Intellectual Life* 6, nos. 3–4:182–92.

Juel, Donald H. 1990. *Mark*. Augsburg Commentary. Minneapolis: Fortress Press.

Keck, Leander E. 1965. "Mark 3:7–12 and Mark's Christology." *Journal of Biblical Literature* 84, no. 4: 341–48.

Kee, Howard Clark. 1977. *Community of the New Age: Studies in the Gospel of Mark*. Philadelphia: Westminster, 1977.

Kelber, Werner H. 1974. *The Kingdom in Mark: A New Place and Time*. Philadelphia: Fortress Press.

Kinukawa, Hisako. 1994. *Women and Jesus in Mark: A Japanese Feminist Perspective*. Maryknoll, NY: Orbis.

LaHaye, Tim F., and Jerry B. Jenkins. 1995-2003. *Left Behind Series*. Carol Stream, IL: Tyndale House Publishers.

Lindsey, Hal, and Carole C. Carson. 1970. *The Late Great Planet Earth*. Grand Rapids: Zondervan.

Maddock, Sherry, and Geoff Maddock. 2007. "An Ever-Renewed Adventure of Faith." In *An Emergent Manifesto of Hope*, edited by Doug Pagitt and Tony Jones, 79–88. Grand Rapids: Baker Books.

Malbon, Elizabeth Struthers. 1986. "Disciples/Crowd/Whoever." *NovT* 28:104–30.

Malbon, Elizabeth Struthers. 1983. "Fallible Followers: Women and Men in the Gospel of Mark." *Semeia* 28:29–48.

Malina, Bruce J. 1993. "Authoritarianism." In *Biblical Social Values and Their Meaning: A Handbook*, edited by John J. Pilch and Bruce Malina. 11–17. Peabody, MA: Hendrickson.

Mann, C. S. 1986. *Mark: A New Translation with Introduction and Commentary*. AB 27. New York: Doubleday.

Marcus, Joel. 1992. "The Jewish War and the *Sitz Im Leben* of Mark." *JBL* 111:441–62.
McLaren, Brian. 2004. *A Generous Orthodoxy*. Cajon, CA: Youth Specialties Books.
Meier, John P. 2000. "The Historical Jesus and the Historical Herodians." *JBL* 119:740–46.
Miller, Susan. 2004. *Women in Mark's Gospel*. New York: T&T Clark.
Mitchell, Henry H. 1990. *Celebration and Experience in Preaching*. Nashville: Abingdon.
Mitchell, Joan L. 2001. *Beyond Fear and Silence: A Feminist-Literary Approach to the Gospel of Mark*. New York: Continuum.
Myers, Ched. 1988. *Binding the Strong Man: A Political Reading of Mark's Story of Jesus*. Maryknoll, NY: Orbis.
Pesch, Rudolf. 1976-80. *Das Markusevangelium*, 2 vols. HTKNT. Freiburg: Herder.
Pilch, John J. 1993. "Power." In *Biblical Social Values and Their Meaning: A Handbook*, edited by John J. Pilch and Bruce Malina. 139–42. Peabody: Hendrickson.
Placher, William C. 2010. *Mark*. Belief: A Theological Commentary on the Bible. Louisville: Westminster John Knox.
Powery, Emerson B. 2007. "Mark." In *True to Our Native Land: An African American New Testament Commentary*, edited by Brian K. Blount, 121–57. Minneapolis: Fortress Press.
Rhoads, David, Joanna Dewey, and Donald Michie. 2012. *Mark as Story: An Introduction to the Narrative of a Gospel*. 3rd ed. Minneapolis: Fortress Press.
Saldarini, Anthony J. 1998. *Pharisees, Scribes, and Sadducees in Palestinian Society*. Grand Rapids: Eerdmans.
Schüssler Fiorenza, Elisabeth. 1992. *But She Said: Feminist Practices of Biblical Interpretation*. Boston: Beacon.
Schweitzer, Albert. 2001. *The Quest for the Historical Jesus: The First Complete Edition*. Trans. and ed. John Bowden. Minneapolis: Fortress Press.
Stone, Lawrence. 1994. "Family Values in a Historical Perspective." Tanner Lectures on Human Values, Harvard University, November 16 and 17.
St. Clair, Raquel A. 2008. *Call and Consequences: A Womanist Reading of Mark*. Minneapolis: Fortress Press.
Theissen, Gerd. 1991. *The Gospels in Context: Social and Political History in the Synoptic Tradition*. Translator Linda M. Maloney. Minneapolis: Fortress Press.

Thomas, Frank A. 1997. *They Like to Never Quit Praisin' God: The Role of Celebration in Preaching.* Cleveland: United Church Press.

Tolbert, Mary Ann. 1989. *Sowing the Gospel: Mark's World in Literary Perspective.* Minneapolis: Fortress Press.

Waetjen, Herman C. 1989. *A Reordering of Power: A Socio-Political Reading of Mark's Gospel.* Minneapolis: Fortress Press.

Weisse, Christian Hermann (1838). *Die evangelische Geschichte kritisch und philosophisch bearbeitet.* Leipzig: Breitkopf und Härtel.

Wilke, Christian Gottlob. 1838. *Der Urevangelist oder exegetisch kritische Untersuchung über das Verwandtschaftsverhältniß der drei ersten Evangelien.* Dresden und Leipzig, G. Fleischer.

Weeden, Theodore. 1971. *Traditions in Conflict.* Philadelphia: Fortress Press.